A Different South Armagh

One woman's story of living between the British Army and the IRA during the Troubles in South Armagh, Northern Ireland

ᴜS

© Copyright 2011
Christine Toner

Published by
Teaghlach Publishing
39 Main Street
Forkhill, Newry
Co. Down
BT35 9SQ

Email: christine@teaghlachpublishing.com
Web: www.adifferentsoutharmagh.com

Published May 2011
Reprinted September 2011

ISBN: 978-0-9568582-0-7

Email: christine@teaghlachpublishing.com
Web: www.adifferentsoutharmagh.com

Foreword

It is my pleasure to write a foreword to this book. I congratulate Christine Toner on her many long hours of putting it all together and creating such a record of life in South Armagh in recent times.

The book, which is well written and structured, chronicles Christine's early years in her native Crossmaglen, the lives and times of the people there in the Fifties and Sixties, the ownership and the lay-out of various businesses and premises, the characters and the pastimes and the daily banter of all who came to her family shop.

It also chronicles the early years of Pat and Christine in England and their return to live and rear their family in Forkhill. It details their commitment to the Civil Rights movement and how they were often in the firing lines of the unfolding conflict as they took the constitutional path to progress.

The book outlines Pat's election to the Newry and Mourne Council where he served the people for a quarter of a century and how as Chairman, 1985-86, he was part of a delegation to Washington in support of the International Fund for Ireland in the build up to the signing of the Anglo Irish Agreement.

I have known Pat and Christine since the Seventies, and like many others I remain uplifted and inspired by their courage, inspiration and noble bearing.

Despite the many trials they endured, despite the pressures inflicted on them throughout the long years of the Troubles, they maintained the constitutional route of peaceful progress that has now largely been adopted by all.

They embodied all that is great and noble in South Armagh, the song tradition and the GAA, recalling Pat's superb contribution to Armagh Minor Side of 1957 where he won an Ulster medal and reached the All Ireland final by defeating Kerry in the semi final of that year. He was also a prominent member of the famous Abbey winning Corn no nOg side of 1954. As singers they performed many of the Irish ballads and popular songs at concerts and functions throughout Ireland.

I recommend this book to all who wish to read of real courage and perseverance. It is a story that needed to be told for the sake of history. As time goes on, it will take on a more and more inspirational dynamic, how Christine and Pat lived and worked and reared their family in Forkhill in the back drop of a difficult time in Irish history, the story of a couple who remain the inspirational and devoted people they have always been.

by Seamus Mallon - Former M.P. Newry and Armagh

Introduction

South Armagh has been notoriously branded as "Bandit Country" for more than four decades. Violence, brutality and fear have been synonymous with life in this border region. Yet there was another South Armagh – a simpler, peaceful place, where life was lived beyond the wretchedness of the Troubles and the complexities of politics.

This is the emotional and heartfelt story of a young girls' experience of life in the Forties and of growing up in Crossmaglen, a rural village nestling among the drumlins of South Armagh, near the border with the south of Ireland.

Her journey records and charts the early aspirations and hopes typical of many young lives during this era. From the pursuit of opportunities for a better life in England, to the crushing loneliness of living in a country where being Irish was not always acceptable.

None of this, however, would compare to the harsh reality facing a family returning to a country embarking on one of the most horrific periods in Northern Ireland's history. For the next 30 years this family, like many other families would experience at first hand, the disruptive and often sinister nature of the notorious Troubles.

Dedication

I dedicate this book to my Son Patrick. He was a precious son whom we sadly lost on the 24th October 2009.

Contents

Chapter 1
GROWING UP IN CROSSMAGLEN

I was raised by my grandparents, Tommy and Annie Clarke, in The Square in Crossmaglen, a village nestling among the drumlins of South Armagh, near the border with the south of Ireland. My grandparents started their little business from their house on The Square, and together they travelled by horse and cart to markets and fairs in neighbouring villages, selling fruit and vegetables. Annie, my grandmother was a woman of great ambition. She worked very hard and thought nothing of going out in all kinds of weather into the quaint little villages that make up South Armagh. It had always been their intention to open their own shop, and when they bought the little house on The Square, which consisted of two rooms upstairs and two rooms downstairs, they set about doing just that.

They divided the front room with a partition, which had a small opening where customers could be served by my grandmother from the opposite side. My grandfather bought the house next door, with the intention of knocking the walls within each house to make one large shop with living accommodation above. My beloved grandfather died before he could fulfil his dream, so my grandmother, with all the love she had for him, carried out his wishes and when the project was completed she was the proud owner of a greengrocer and confectioners shop combined with living accommodation on the top floor. This was the hub of the village. People dropped in daily, if only to report on the weather, discuss the headlines in the daily Irish Press or inform my grandmother of a recently deceased member of the community.

The interior of the shop was painted white, with wooden shelves fitted to the walls behind a big wooden counter top. Each of the shelves were carefully stacked with food items such as tea; sugar, flour, eggs, jars of sweets, boxes of Cadbury's Roses Milk Tray, Quality Street and an assortment of fruit and cigarettes. On the opposite side of the shop was a large wooden bench where boxes of potatoes, carrots, onions, cabbages, cauliflower and various other kinds of vegetables were displayed. Even today I can still see the vibrancy in colour of those beautifully displayed fresh vegetables, bursting with goodness. There was, of course, no comparison to the big supermarkets of today, but everything in that shop was fresh, bought from the markets in Belfast early every morning and when one considers it was the late Forties and early Fifties, this was a great achievement in itself. Not many people had their own cars and only a few years earlier my granny and granddad travelled from village to village by pony and cart.

Most evenings I would stand in the doorway of my home and gaze across that Square, surrounded by this magical place with its colourful buildings, painted with great care and attention. It gave me a sense of belonging to one very large family in a Crossmaglen where everyone knew each other and looked out for their neighbours. As my grandmother said to me many times "The largest Square in Ireland, and we should all be very proud of it" And of course we were. Crossmaglen Square was very well known throughout the length and breadth of Ireland. No matter where you went and during conversation, if you mentioned you came from Crossmaglen, people would remark, "Oh yes! We have heard of that place". They always acknowledged how friendly the people were and of the large Square where the Fair was held on the first Friday of each month. People came to the Fair in "Cross" as it was affectionately known, from far and wide, especially from across the border. There were horse dealers who travelled from Carrickmacross, Ballybay, Kingscourt, Castleblayney, and as far away as Kerry, Connemara and Galway.

Then, aged ten years and standing in the doorway of my home, looking across The Square, I knew every house and business and I can still picture in my mind each one exactly as it was then. My home was on the west side of The Square, and to the left was North Street, which was the route to Castleblayney in Co. Monaghan. To the right, and passing our door was a continuation of the road, which led to the top of the town and onto the Dundalk Road, which eventually brought you to

Dundalk. Directly across the road and on the left hand side was the northern part of The Square.

The first building was known as the billiard room, which was used by American and English soldiers during the Second World War. These soldiers were billeted in lands a short distance away on the Newry Road where they performed manoeuvres while awaiting dispatch orders.

Next-door was Martin's, the newsagents and confectioners, where local people gathered every morning to collect the newspaper and exchange their favourite bits of gossip. Instead of going home many of the men would open the paper and start to read it on the street, checking the times of the race meetings and picking out the name of a horse, whilst deciding whether to place a bet or not. Usually a small crowd would gather and from time to time chat and laughter would ring out as some of the contents of the newspapers were revealed.

Patrick Martin reared chickens and sold eggs to the egg merchants. To me, he was simply known as the "Egg Man". There were a lot of egg merchants in those days and they came on bikes to collect the eggs, most of them with little wooden trailers attached to the back. The money received was minimal, but the extra income was always useful for a rainy day and anyway it was always good to have a little sideline. Next to Martin's was Carragher's butchers shop, another family business, run by two brothers, one very jovial and the other very quiet. The jovial one was very good at keeping the customers entertained whilst their order was being sorted. Shin beef for making soup to which vegetables could be added; brisket was another popular choice, as well as chops and neck of lamb. I can't remember much steak being bought except for a special treat, and of course a roast was only ever for a very special occasion.

I will always remember one morning, whilst on an errand for my grandmother, a recently wed young man stood in the butcher's shop being quizzed about how he and his wife were now finding married life. Around the time of his wedding, Daz washing powder had just been introduced onto the market along with an advertisement and slogan which went "it's new, it's blue, and it does wonders for you". He was asked how his new wife was keeping and replied by telling everyone in the shop she was pregnant and added, "she's doing well; she washed her knickers in Daz and its done wonders for her." Of course everyone in the shop roared with laughter but when I went home and related the story to my grandmother, I didn't get the same kind of response. There were many other stories I wanted to repeat but the thought of her left hook or the slap of a wet dishcloth around my legs taught me to be more careful about repeating the jokes and stories I had heard.

Next door to Carragher's butchers was the Hibernian Bank. The manager was a Mr. Quinn, a lovely gentleman, and as my Auntie Josie was his housekeeper, I was often brought along with her for company. It was a large house and my auntie did not like being alone in it. Mr. Quinn lived on the second floor above the bank, which was about three stories high. It was a lovely old building with lots of character. Inside it was decorated to such a high degree that you would think you were in a very posh hotel. Mr. Quinn was a single man who at that time had what was considered a very extravagant hobby, horse riding. In the evenings, after tea, he would put on his riding outfit, jodhpurs, boots, jacket and hat, take his whip, saddle his horse and go riding around The Square. Many would say he looked a bit silly, but he loved his horse and would ride out along the country roads oblivious to what others were thinking. Crossmaglen was a great place for horses. Made famous by the Kernan family who bred horses for show jumping and other purposes. It was mostly a town where working horses were brought in from the country to get shod by the local blacksmith, so as you can imagine the sight of Mr. Quinn, riding his horse so gracefully and elegantly to indulge his hobby was considered something of an oddity. Although we did have the pleasure of the Newry Harriers who would come on their annual hunt outing, which was held every September. They would get permission from various landowners to use their land and it was always a lovely sight to see, as the horses and hounds set out through the fields of South Armagh. Crossmaglen had a mixed community and religion was respected regardless of a person's denomination.

Next door to the bank was Loane's draper and outfitter and true to the description on the shop's sign, they sold 'everything you could want for women, men and children'. It was a terrific shop. The interior was very big with large old-fashioned counters. George Loane lived with his wife in an adjoining house overlooking The Square. The shop had full length glass windows and of course glass doors and when you walked inside it seemed to go on forever. The footwear was at the very back of the shop and everything else was organised towards the front, on both sides. The office was on an elevated platform, high up from the floor and completely covered with glass. The shop assistant could be seen inside as she sat high above everything else in the building. As well as looking after the accounts she had control of the cash. The apparatus used to work the transfer of a purchase around the shop fascinated us as children. From each department in the shop were lines with little round containers. Each container could be sent straight to the elevated office, so when something was bought at the counter, the assistant would write out a little docket with the price of the item and the money was put into a container. The assistant then closed the top and pulled a little holder at the end and the container whizzed along the line to the office, where the lady would remove the docket and the money, mark the docket paid and despatch again together with the change back along the line. As children we were mesmerised by such a contraption and after school, from outside the glass fronted facade, we would spend many hours watching these little articles whizzing up and down the shop.

As well as the whizzers, there were other things which caught our attention. Two shop assistants, one a man and the other a lady were clearly attracted to one another. He was responsible for the department at the back of the shop but on frequent occasions he would be found at the ladies counter near the front. It was clear from the outset a game was being played, trying to pass each other behind the counter. This meant he could pretend to get stuck and would only move after he had received a kiss from his blushing lady friend. We would watch them for ages but would not dare tell our parents, as we feared another stinging clout from the dishcloth.

The house next door belonged to Mr and Mrs Donaghy. They had three children. Two of them, Rita and Colette were very good friends of mine and I spent many happy hours in that house with their family. Their father was a welfare officer. He was also the school attendance officer. I remember having mumps and being off school for two weeks and as it was policy that if you had been off school for any length of time the attendance officer would call out your name in front of the entire class and you had to go up to him and explain why you were off. I never had much trouble with him as he knew me well because of my friendship with his girls, and even though he could be a bit scary at times, he was a nice man and so were his wife and family

Next door to the Donaghy's were the offices of Maurice O'Connor, the solicitor. He was a very distinguished gentleman and always had an air of importance about him. He always arrived at his office dressed in black coat, bowler hat, umbrella, and of course the briefcase. He seldom spoke on the street if you met him, but then again as children we dare not speak at all.

The large Post Office was next to the solicitor's office and was run by Mr and Mrs Malcomson. The lady was postmistress and her husband helped her to run a grocery and confectionery business as well as the Post Office. They were a very kind couple and ran their business very well. When they first came to Crossmaglen from Lisnaskea, they fell in love with the place and its people and decided to stay until their retirement from the business. A relative of theirs also opened a pharmacy in the opposite side of the large building. Mr and Mrs Bryson had come to Crossmaglen as a young married couple and continued their successful business for many years. They had two children who went on to university, and regretfully they made the decision to move further north of the province to be near their family.

Along the east side of The Square, where the main Newry Road continued through the actual Square, connecting each area of the town, was an old disused building at the corner. I remember my grandmother telling me about a tragedy that had happened where a little boy accidentally died and how the family were so distraught that they closed their business down. When we were small we were very scared to pass it because an owl took up residence there and at night he would make strange sounds. The dreary old building itself did not help as it was so run down that its doors creaked with the slightest gust of wind and the shutters on the windows rocked from side to side as they beat against the stone walls echoing through the empty building. Of course our imaginations created all sorts of images and to us it became the "haunted house."

Another old building stood next to that one and belonged to Miss Mc Cormack, a quaint old lady who could scare the wits out of you with just one quick look. She didn't use the house, which had railings around it, and the fact that it was not lived in gave it a ghostly look. In the garden stood two massive green palm trees and this added to the scary appearance of the house. The windows reflected the light in a way that gave the impression of someone standing in the shadows looking out. On Easter Sunday people would take palm from the trees on their way to Mass and have it blessed, as was the custom. One Easter Saturday night as a group of us were walking past, there was a notorious rattle and we ran as fast as our legs could carry us. We later found out that the rattle was a hatchet falling from the trees where a few local boys thought if they cut the palm the night before they could sell it to the people going to Mass on Easter Sunday.

Miss Mc Cormack heard about it and she soon found the culprits and brought them to task. She was a formidable lady. Just looking into her eyes you became almost hypnotized and would do anything to get away from her. She always dressed in black with her grey hair tied back in a bun. A stern looking person. Although she lived alone she could handle herself very well and that applied to anyone who stood in her way. She had a business on the far end of The Square and had a few nice people who worked for her in the shop, but as children, she was one lady we tried to avoid. I was often sent to her shop for some particular item, and as mistakes can be made, I might come back home with either the wrong change or the wrong message so I was sent back. I hated having to go back into her shop and have her serve me again and any time I was sent back for some reason, I would stand outside and wait until one of the girls came to the counter, then I would rush in hoping to be served by the girl, but Miss Mc Cormack was there in a flash and the very look on her face would make me forget what I forgot in the first place. Often I left her shop trembling.

Towering over the house with the palm trees stood the Belfast Bank. This was a building I always admired. It stood high and serene, its best feature being two great attic windows in the roof that overlooked The Square. I always wanted to get up there and look out over The Square because it was the one place to get the perfect view. The bank itself was on the ground floor with the living accommodation on various floors above and as it was private I could only dream about the view from the upstairs windows. It was many years later before I got the chance to view The Square from those windows and as the years went on that same view would be used for more sinister reasons.

The shop next to the bank belonged to Peter Harvey or "The Popes" as it was called. Peter and his wife sold religious items in their lovely little shop and the two of them would go around the churches when a Mission was on. He set up his stall outside the chapel and sold various religious items such as rosary beads, holy pictures, medals, statues and prayer books etc. Each parish had a Mission in those days about every three years, lasting for two weeks and the whole community attended Mass every morning and evening.

Mass in the morning was at six thirty to accommodate the people going to work and again at eight to suit those at home, and in the evening a final mass at eight o'clock. All attended the sermon, which was given of course by the priests of the Missionary Order who were visiting. During those two weeks, religion was very much to the fore. If you were a lapsed Catholic this was your chance to repent and start all over again. Apart from the religious aspect it was also a wonderful opportunity for country people to come from neighbouring parishes and meet people whom they may not have seen since the previous Mission. Of course many people repented and started again only to stop as soon as the Mission ended, but people did pack the chapel for two weeks and listened attentively to the sermons, which were based on the many day to day and night time happenings going on at the time. These included missing mass on Sundays and holy days, not going to confession, talking about your neighbours, spreading evil gossip, stealing, being in debt, reading dirty books, keeping bad company and of course, being under the influence of alcohol. Today as I write these memories I am thinking how much times have changed. Sitting listening to those sermons did prick our consciences and if you had done something wrong you would repent and try to lead a better life.

The house next to "The Popes" was Harry Cumiskey's. He and his wife had a large family. Josephine Cumiskey was one of my classmates at school, and became very ill at the age of nine. I shall never forget that day at school when our teacher told us that she had died. We were the same age and I know I cried so much for her because, like all of us, we had dreams of doing wonderful things when we grew up and now she was never going to get that chance. The teacher told us all that we were to walk out to Connor's Hill. I mentioned Mr O'Connor earlier; he lived in a beautiful big house with a long driveway that was surrounded by many acres of land which you entered through gates at the top of the hill. That part of the road was known as Connor's Hill, about half a mile outside Crossmaglen on the Newry Road. When someone died in the hospital and the remains were coming home, the local people would walk to Connor's Hill and wait for the hearse with the remains and accompany it to the chapel. That was my first sad walk to meet a funeral. It was also the start of many more sad funerals.

Cumiskey's was next door to Mrs McCabe. A dressmaker, she was a widow with one child. I ran across The Square so many times to her house in my young days when my grandmother sent me with whatever needed to be mended. She would bring me in and sit me down in her room while she checked to see if it was a small job or a large one, and would always do it immediately so I could wait. She was a very gentle person and I often wondered how she had the patience to do her work looking at the material spread out across the table with just her and a little sewing machine. But she took it all in her stride.

Mc Cusker's next door was a hairdressing salon. Two sisters, Molly and Bridie worked in the ladies salon on the second floor of the building, while their brother Peter- or Pete as he was known- worked in the barber's shop on the ground floor. Another brother, John drove a taxi which in those days was a good business to have. Mc Cuskers was the place where every day happenings were discussed. It was always busy and the men had great craic while waiting for a haircut or a shave. Pete, who used a cut-throat razor, was well known for being a good barber and giving a good shave. This was a straight razor where the barber skilfully slides the razor along the face and removes the beard. The same as today, except now you can have hot towels applied to the face and very luxurious lotion. Pete was a great football supporter and on the Sunday when a match was on, especially a big match such as an All-Ireland final from Croke Park, he would bring his radio outside and place it on the windowsill, turn the sound up as high as possible and you would hear the match being broadcast all over The Square.

The two girls upstairs had a very busy hairdressing salon and I honestly think it was in that salon that I had my first inspiration to become a hairdresser. I did Irish dancing at school and later when I left primary school, an Irish dancing teacher came to Crossmaglen once every week to teach dancing. For many years I took lessons with her as did other girls and boys, and we took part in all the Feiseanna throughout the area. I won quite a few medals for my dancing and so whenever a local concert or play was performed, some of the children would dance during the interval and for that occasion I would get my hair put in curls so it would be nice and bouncy when I danced. When there was a concert on I would go to McCusker's to get my hair done. I never wanted to leave it because they would let me help with handing the clips and curlers, and I loved every minute of it. My grandmother would have to send someone to get me or come herself.

There was always great craic in the hairdressers and you were sure to get the up-to-date news on whatever was happening around the town. Trainor's- or Chums- as it was known was next, but separated by the Mill Lane which led to the back of the buildings on that side of The Square. It also ran along each side to connect with the Newry Road and the Monug Road towards the graveyard, and the local chapel. There was always something very secretive about the Mill Lane and we were warned not to go down there but as children that is where we went during the summer days. We climbed the wall at the end of the lane and went into the graveyard and would walk around reading the writings on the tombstones. The every day routine was going into the chapel to say a prayer and then we would go up on to the front gallery, which was out of bounds to children unless they sang in the choir. The front gallery accommodated the choir and was sealed off from the seats where the congregation sat during Mass. At the back of the gallery and to the side was a little door which lead into the belfry and sometimes during a choir practice the sexton came to ring the bell for the Angelus. He would open the door slightly and slip in. He never opened it wide enough to see in and of course our curiosity got the better of us, so this area had to be explored and what better time to do this only during the summer holidays.

This was our priority, and on the gallery we proceeded through the belfry door. We were starting to lose our courage, when we decided we would all push together and as we did the door sprang open to reveal a life size statue of the Crucifixion with the crown of thorns on his head. This frightened the life out of us. We thought we had seen an apparition. We ran from that gallery and none of us remember our feet ever touching the stairs on the way down. We decided to stick to reading the writings on tombstones after that. One evening just as it was starting to get dark we found a particular headstone. That read "I am not dead just sleeping here". We all took off as fast as we could and that ended our visits down the Mill Lane and into the graveyard!

Bikes were repaired and punctures fixed in Chum's shop while his Sister Mary ran the pub, which was in another part of the building. This part of The Square was always a hive of activity with people always coming and going either to the pub, the bicycle shop, the barbers or the hairdressers. The next building was known as the Market House and it took priority over all the other buildings on The Square. The lower part on the ground floor housed the two buses, which provided public transport into Newry, either to get to work, for shopping, or just for a day out. Days out however were very rare then, and apart from getting to work the only other reasons were perhaps to visit the dentist or the hospital. Of course often a trip into Newry did mean a day out because it involved getting the early bus, getting off on the Mall where the bus stop was, then walking down Monaghan Street and up to Daisy Hill Hospital, waiting to be called for the appointment, walking all that way down the hill again. Maybe just have enough time for a look at the shops or get a cup of tea. Then it was time to get the bus home again and indeed in those days many people did not have much time on their hands or have the money to spend a whole day in Newry.

In the old days the Market House in Crossmaglen held a local market once a week and on the top floor was a very big hall. I remember my grandmother telling me about going to dances there in her young days. As I listened to the stories she told me about how they would dance the night away into the early hours of the morning and then sneak into their beds. I often thought what a wonderful time they seemed to have. They had very little money and very few of them ever tasted alcohol but they all enjoyed themselves in a very innocent way. In later years the Market House became a cinema. Not a very elaborate one but I do remember going as a child, when the hard seats at the front were known as the nine pennies and the slightly more comfortable seats were the one and six pennies. (In today's money nine old pence was about four pence and one and six pence was about seven and a half pence) but I saw some great films!

There was a brilliant drama group based in Crossmaglen with Eva Cassidy as the producer. Her wonderful cast members of the group performed some of the best plays staged here.

Keenan's pub was next door and then a house, which belonged to Kernan's. It was rented out to Mr. and Mrs Dowds and they lived there with their two little boys. Mr Dowds was a policeman in the barracks at that time. This was not unusual because a lot of policemen lived in rented houses. The single men lived in the barracks but the married policemen with their families lived throughout the town. Ramie Dowds was a brilliant footballer. As a young boy at school in Crossmaglen he played on the local team and in later years played for Co. Armagh Minor Team.

Mrs Callaghan's was next door. She had a small grocery and confectioners shop and it was here at night we would all meet outside to get our sweets and soft drinks before going to the pictures. Although

I could have got my own sweets from my Grannies shop, it was always a novelty getting them with my friends. Next to Callaghan's were the two McArdle sisters, who owned a shoe shop and when you went there to buy shoes they smothered you with attention and what should have taken less than half an hour to purchase a pair of shoes would take half a day. They just loved to hear the news from around the town and every time you were about to leave, some other story cropped up. That was it for another hour.

Leaving the east side and onto the south side of The Square stood O'Donnell's pub where the proprietor Bill O'Donnell lived with his wife and sons. Bill was a Justice of the Peace. A pleasant gentleman with a kind nature who would go out of his way to help people and he was well respected by everyone.

Although he held a very prominent position in Cross, he made everyone welcome and did whatever he could to help anyone who approached him. No matter what the problem was he always made himself available to help in whatever way he could. Next door to Bill was Jodler Hughes' pub. The Hughes' were a respected family and one of his nephews attended school with me.

Mrs McKenna and her son Frankie had a small business next door to Hughes'. She was a seamstress and her son a tailor; a very nice little lady and I spent some time with her, as her granddaughter Josephine Fitzpatrick was my best friend. While playing with her granddaughter, I watched how Mrs McKenna moved her little fingers pushing the needle and thread so neatly as she stitched hems and turned collars on shirts. For in those days the collars on shirts were doubled, and when they got very worn around the neck, the collar was first removed then reversed to produce a whole new collar. This prolonged the life of the shirt for many a man for another few months.

Mc Shanes was the next house. Indeed many times I went to Mc Shanes with a little galvanised can to get milk, as a lot of people in the town did.

Paddy had a herd of milking cows and every evening they were brought in from the field. You could set a clock to the exact time they would come down the road in a line, not one bit unruly, and shuffled out the back to be milked in the byre. Local people went there to collect milk for themselves.

A milkman came to the schools from Newtownhamilton to deliver little bottles of milk for the children and I remember on cold days the teachers would put the crates of milk beside the fire to heat them and sometimes they would get so hot that the little silver top caps would burst open with the heat.

The next house was Robbie McAllisters. He was a cobbler with a big family and one of their daughters, Rose, was also my school friend. I made many trips to that part of the Square in my youth, if not for milk, then it was to get shoes mended or clothes altered.

Josie Martin's pub was the last building on that side of The Square. A quiet little pub with its own customers like all the others.

The west side of The Square was across the Dundalk Road where the Technical School stood in its own grounds surrounded by railings at the sides and a large secure gate at the front. Many young people went there after leaving primary school especially those who did not pass the qualifying exam. A child who did pass this exam would get a full scholarship to attend a Grammar school. In a lot of cases parents who could afford to pay the fees for their children could do so but the children had to complete an entrance exam first, and if they passed they were accepted. This later became known as the Eleven Plus.

Next to the Tech was the Morgan family. The father was a Blacksmith who worked extremely hard and sometimes late into the night. He and his wife were rearing a large family in very difficult times. Their boys grew up to be famous Gaelic football players and in later years the grandchildren carried on their legacy and became famous players with Crossmaglen Rangers and Co. Armagh Gaelic football team. The family, who lived next door to them were hard working people. They suffered a terrible loss; a train tragically killed their son as he walked along the railway line. He was a friend of my Uncle Tom and this tragic loss affected the family very much.

The house next door belonged to the Grants, Felix, an Irish step dancer, was so agile that he lived well into his eighties. His family was small in comparison to much of the larger families in Crossmaglen but they were very talented people. His son was brilliant at playing the banjo, and of course in a community like Crossmaglen in those days, it was lovely to see father and son do their party piece, which they both did for years.

Mc Namee's bakery next door was a hub of activity where people gathered in the early morning to get the first batch of freshly baked bread. Loaves with their crust still warm. Soda farls and scones, pancakes and wheaten bread, all so light and crumbly, waiting for the spread of lovely fresh butter. The smell of bread baking was all across The Square and even though times were difficult we were assured of fresh bread.

Quigley's pub was next door and beside that a little shop rented by a lovely lady, Miss Quinn, who was brilliant at lacework. When I went to her shop for a message I would watch her work and if she was in the process of finishing off a piece she would make you wait until she had it finished. I never minded having to wait because I loved to watch her skilled hands as she would stitch the intricate little shamrock on the lace.

Miss McCormick was next door, a woman who scared the life out of me every time I went into her shop. Then next door was Jack Mc Entee's butchers or "Jack's Hut" as it was known locally. A little hut spotlessly clean and the best of meat was sold there. Jack was a true gentleman. As we grew older we found that behind Jack's Hut was a great courting place on our way home from the dances in the Rangers Hall.

Across the road- the Culloville Road, was Murphy's garage. One of two garages in Crossmaglen. Next door was a house that belonged to Mc Conville's and it was here that my best friend Josephine from my younger days lived with her family. The red telephone kiosk, which housed the public phone, was just outside the front door, and around this little house there was always plenty of activity as people waited on phone calls from loved ones who were in England or America. Some waited until the box was free to make phone calls to many destinations. In those days very few households had a telephone so this was the only way people could communicate.

A large gateway leading to the yard separated that house from Mc Conville' s shop and house. It was at Mc Conville's house and yard that I can recall the happiest times of my life. Mc Conville's was a general store and a very large business. They were suppliers to farmers and in those days there was a very large farming community around South Armagh. As well as having the shop, they were the local undertakers, as well as doing a bit of farming. Their cattle were brought in from the outskirts of the town to be milked every evening. Mr and Mrs Mc Conville had five children. One boy and four girls. Almost every day after school I ran to their house to play with the children and their friends. They had a very large yard with many, many outhouses and a large loft where you had to climb a lot of steps to gain access. Once inside it was a wonderland for a child's imagination, a place where every impossible dream could come true. There were bags of meal, oats, all the stuff farmers would use and at one side of the loft was a trap door which allowed the person in charge to lower by chains and a pulley, whatever animal feed a farmer needed.

The farmer could drive his tractor and trailer directly under the trap door so that as the door opened the bags would be lowered onto the trailer. As children we jumped through those trap doors onto bags of meal on the trailer and also into hay on the way through to be stored in larger sheds at the back of the yard for animal feed during the winter. Whenever the hay was cut and stacked in the field just outside the town, it was then brought in to be stored, the hay slide was drawn by two beautiful black mares When it got to the field, the back of the slide was tipped down and slid under the hay stack and thus the hay was guided up onto the hay slide by chains, and there, it started its journey on the road back to the yard. When it was unloaded the slide went back to the field to collect the next stack of hay and all the children would jump on the slide on these return journeys. To this very day, I can remember the crowds of children that were on that slide and see the others running after it to get on, reaching out their hands for the children already on the slide to pull them on.

Down at the very back of the loft in a secluded place was where the coffins were kept. They were actually made in the loft by a tradesman and we played hide and seek around the bags of meal. On many occasions we hid in the coffins and put the lid on to make sure we had a good hiding place. We thought very little of it then. To us it was fun, but later in life we would realize that coffins and funerals were to become symbols of hatred and great tragedy.

Paul Mc Geough's shop was next to McConville's and he and his sisters ran a drapery shop. Again, I spent a lot of time in that shop just going in and looking around and the girls would start giving me little jobs to do.

A family called Wilsons, a protestant family, owned the house next door. This was not unusual in Crossmaglen when I was growing up. In the Wilson family there were two girls and one boy, and we all played together as children. Religion never was a problem. They were nice people and we had great times together.

This brings me back to my grandmother's, but first there is one more house to mention to complete The Square, our next-door neighbours on the north side, Cumiskey's. This was a big shop and they sold everything, grocery, fruit, bacon, eggs, tea, and sugar and so on. My grandmother and Johnny Cumiskey were in opposition to each other for years, sometimes they gave the impression that they did not get on but it was all an act, they competed very well together and looking back now it was absolutely wonderful to have watched them compete.

Friday was the fish day and herrings were the catch of the day. Many boxes of herrings were bought and these were sat outside the shops and people came along and looked and bought, Granny outside her shop and Johnny outside his shop. He had a great voice and so shouted "Herrings alive with their eyes opened, pipes in their mouths and them all smoking". Now and again he would shout to her, "Annie! Will you have lodgers tonight? Meaning she might be left with fish, and she would shout back to him "Keep shouting Johnny. You shout and I'll sell". There were of course other parts of Crossmaglen equally well known. There were more pubs and many more shops apart from those on The Square but I am describing where I lived and what it was like when I was growing up. Kind hearted people who would do you a good turn if they could. And so as the years rolled quickly by I found myself about to leave primary school and go on to secondary school

I first met Pat Toner in my grandmother's shop in the summer of 1956. My Auntie Kathleen who had ran the shop for Granny and who was her youngest daughter was getting married. I did not go back to school after the summer holidays but started to work in the shop. Pat was a student at the Abbey Grammar School in Newry and during the summer holidays he worked for John Haughey of Forkhill, who was a Solicitor, and had offices in Newry and Crossmaglen. Mr Haughey, also owned a grain mill and a large farm, and during the summer months supplied limestone to farmers for spreading on their land. Pat lived in Forkhill and his particular job that summer was selling lime to farmers in South Armagh and indeed sometimes he had to help in the spreading of the lime by driving a lime spreader. Pat also played Gaelic football and his reputation at the Abbey as a footballer was outstanding. He was also playing for the Co. Armagh Minor Team. As he was so well known by most of the farmers in the area this meant he was able to sell a lot of lime, and as there was a government subsidy on the lime it was pretty cheap. Pat recalls that the selling price of lime that year 1956-57 was 14 shillings a tonne spread. In today's money 70 pence. Pat was on very little wages but his commission was 1 shilling per tonne. In today's money 5 pence. He sold hundreds of tonnes of lime and ended up earning a lot more money than the manager of the business. This did not last too long and his commission was soon changed from 1 shilling per tonne (5 pence in today's money) to 2 pennies per tonne. Even then, Pat earned enough money to afford to buy a second hand car and he became very popular with a lot of young people in the village because he could take them to places like Dundalk, Newry and Warrenpoint and he had money to spend.

On the day I met Pat I had been cleaning the shop window outside and was not aware of the young man sitting in a van outside Cumiskey's shop next door. Later on he came into the shop to buy a packet of cigarettes and I served him, gave him his change, thanked him and he was gone. An hour later he came back. Seemingly he had given me £1 note and I had only given him change of a ten-shilling note, which that time was equivalent to fifty pence except that it was then paper money. I was very embarrassed. We did not have a till in those days but a money drawer with several compartments for coins and notes. I did not even check as to whether I did or did not make a mistake. I just opened the drawer gave him the change and wished he would go away quickly, but he didn't. Instead he gave me a half crown which is about twenty-five pence in today's money, he said it was for myself and hoped that this would not cause me any trouble at the end of the day when the money would be counted. Pat did not know then that I actually lived there and that my grandmother owned the shop.

Sundays were busy days in our shop. In those days there were two Masses on Sunday. First Mass was at eight o'clock and second Mass was at eleven o'clock. Our shop opened after first Mass and stayed open until late at night when the cinema closed, usually by eleven to half eleven. There would be a football match in Crossmaglen Rangers' field every Sunday and various teams came and battled it out. Culloville was one of the teams. Tough men of course and also Mullaghbawn and Forkhill to mention a few. We would all go to first Mass on Sunday which was at eight o' clock in the morning and when we came home we had our breakfast. My granny started her extra batch of ice cream. It was always busy after Mass and especially after the later eleven o' clock Mass. However, apart from this, Sunday was busy for another reason. After the football match all the players would gather in our shop for ice cream and minerals. There was a huge bench at the end of the shop where all would sit, eating their ice cream and drinking minerals and indeed many a match was replayed there. Johnny Brannigan from Camlough had a taxi and drove most teams for the County Board to wherever their matches were to take place. A very quiet spoken man, he was a great character. You don't drive a group of young men around from week to week he would say, without getting to know them and their little secrets. Johnny was familiar with our shop as he always stopped before leaving Crossmaglen with whatever team he had.

On this particular Sunday he was driving a group of young footballers for Armagh Minor trials in Crossmaglen and after the match the team arrived in the shop for the usual ice cream and drinks.

He always stayed at the counter with his arms folded and surveyed his merry band of young men. I was a fifteen-year-old girl with long blond hair, which in itself was an attraction, and standing behind a counter facing up to twenty young men on the other side, you can imagine what the various comments were. Yes, dates were asked for and promises were made.

They were all going to be in Crossmaglen Hall that night and if I were there I would get a dance or two. Slowly and quietly Johnny said "Boys you will all be there, but I know that there is only one man here who will have any chance of dancing this young girl tonight" He pointed to the corner of the bench. Everyone looked over and there was Pat Toner sitting quietly, not saying a word. Obviously Johnny knew more than he was letting on. As for me, I had not even noticed he was there.

Those dances in Crossmaglen Hall were every Sunday night, but every second Sunday there was a Ceili with old time Irish dancing and some old time waltzes. I was allowed to go on the second Sunday as these finished a little earlier than the normal dances. The Ceili and Old Time just so happened to be on that Sunday night that Forkhill and Culloville had played and I was going. Always after a good match, and especially if there had been a wee bit of agro, some slagging would go on as the players were leaving the field.

"Oh you'll not be as big a man Toner when you are on your own in Cross tonight" or "I wonder will you have so much to say tonight in Cross".

Crossmaglen Rangers Hall was very popular on Sunday nights, and no matter what was said leaving the field there never was any trouble and everyone enjoyed themselves. I can honestly say that in those days Crossmaglen was the place to live and grow up in. Pat was in Crossmaglen that Sunday night and he danced me most of the night. I suppose that was when the romance really started. I was 15 and he was17, and when he walked me home that night we said goodnight but we did not make plans to meet again.

I was very young and I could never be sure if I would be allowed to go to the Hall every time the Ceili and Old Time was on for a lot depended then on how well I worked during the week and on how well I had behaved. Although I lived in Grannies, my mother and father were still close at hand and kept a close watch on what I did and where I went.

When September came Pat did not want to return to the Abbey Grammar School. After working all summer and having extra money and the car. One week after the new school term began, his parents had a visit from one of the teachers from the Abbey, a Brother Rehill to find out why Pat did not go back at the start of term. After speaking for about an hour Pat's parents made him promise Brother Rehill that he would return to school the following Monday. Pat played on the Abbey football team from he first went there. He loved football and was on the team when the Abbey won the Corn na nOg Cup in 1954, when they beat St Pat's CBS Cavan. Pat maintained the young player that he marked that day was Sean Brady who is now our Cardinal. Pat always insisted, when his mother tried to persuade him to go back to the Abbey that it wasn't for his brains they wanted him, but for his football ability. On Monday morning Pat took his school bag and left home to go to school, but instead went to Haughey's and continued to work there for a month or so. He then left there and got a job at Quinn's of the Milestone in Newry.

Pat also played on the Co. Armagh Minor Team which won the Ulster Championship in 1957 and went on to get to the All- Ireland final in Croke Park but Armagh Minors were defeated in the final by Meath. Pat holds medals for Corn Na nOg, Ulster, and an All- Ireland runner up medal. He also played football on The Milestone football team, which included Kevin O'Neill, Tony Haden and Tom McKay. Kevin and Tony went on to play for the Co. Down Senior Team, which was the first Gaelic football team to take the Sam Maguire across the border to the North.

Chapter 2
SMUGGLER

Crossmaglen, in my childhood and teenage years, was a wonderful place to live and I have many happy memories of growing up there. It was a busy town being close to the border and a lot of southern people came across the border to shop. The Fair Day in Cross was a big day. In those days there were pigs, horses, cattle and sheep as well as stalls with clothes and some new and second-hand furniture. There was also entertainment. I will always remember Maggie Barry singing and playing her banjo in Cross Fair and how the crowds would gather around and listen to her for hours. Maggie Barry was a street singer who lived outside Crossmaglen and who travelled throughout Ireland singing at Fairs. Some years later Maggie Barry was spotted by a talent scout and brought to England and then to America where she sang in Carnegie Hall in New York, where only the very best entertain. She stayed and entertained in America for a number of years.

At that time there were customs' huts at the border and their cars scouted the unapproved roads. The Police patrolled the streets day and night and also patrolled the countryside on bicycles. Crossmaglen was a haven for smugglers as almost every road led to the border. In order to drive into the south of Ireland from the North each car owner was issued with a book entitled "Temporary Importation of Private Motor Cars and Motor Cycles, Record of Entries and Exits". There were different frontier posts. Coming from Crossmaglen we would use the post at Drumbilla and on arrival at the customs post the driver stopped, got out of the car, brought the book into the hut where it was stamped by an officer at the space which showed 'entry'. The stamp in red showed "Customs and Excise, Frontier Post, Date, Drumbilla, Dundalk. The same thing applied coming back except that the stamp showed in the space of 'exit'. The customs hut opened early in the morning and remained open until nine thirty or ten o'clock at night. For people going into the South for a night's entertainment, which the majority of people living along the border towns did in those days, a request could be made with the officer on duty. The driver gave a time when he would be returning to the north, and so the officer on duty would stay on until that time to stamp the book with the date and time returned.

As well as Dundalk there was Castleblayney and Carrickmacross. Great towns for shopping and entertainment as most things were cheaper in the South, including cigarettes, alcohol and clothes. To go to Carrickmacross via the hut or frontier was a roundabout way, as first one had to go to Tullydonnell and get a book stamped and then travel via Roche, Iniskeen and on to Carrickmacross. To go to Castleblayney was about the same. Living in Crossmaglen as I did, we travelled a lot to Dundalk but mostly to Carrickmacross. My uncle, a horse dealer lived there and my grandfather and he worked together, travelling all around the country to Fairs where they would buy and sell horses. I remember well some very enjoyable trips to Carrick in a pony and trap with my grandfather and my granny. He had a great liking for horses and a great way with them. Of his four sons, I think it was my Uncle Mick in Carrick who was the only one that shared granddad's love of horses. My last journey to Carrick by pony and trap was when I was seven years old. My other uncles: Tom, Neilus and Paddy had cars, which Granddad enjoyed too but as more and more cars were on the roads it had become too busy and dangerous for the horses.

To go to Dundalk, Castleblayney and Carrickmacross, travelling the unapproved roads saved a driver those extra few miles and time. Every road out of Cross was an unapproved road. The Dundalk Road, the Monug Road, the Culloville Road. This road did have customs huts, one north and one south, the Blayney Road and the Glassdrummond Road. These had no customs huts and to travel to any of the southern towns via these roads was referred to locally as "jumping the border".

Indeed, as a little girl it took me a long time to understand how a car or lorry could jump the border. But jump they did, and as I got older our journeys were also made in the same way. I am sure that many a customs officer sat out a late request at Tullydonnell waiting for a car to return when in fact those who made the request were at home in their beds fast asleep after jumping the border. The worst thing that could happen to a driver travelling the unapproved roads was to be caught or overtaken by the customs car, which patrolled all those roads. Indeed many a good chase took place along those roads in South Armagh, Brands Hatch could not compare with the skill of some of those drivers! It was worse if there was a bit of smuggling going on and I am sure almost everyone in South Armagh at some time in his or her life did a bit of smuggling! If you bought anything in the South, for example, a pair of shoes or jewellery or maybe something for the house and brought them back to the North, this was classed as smuggling. Worse still, if stopped by the customs they could confiscate your goods and you risked losing your car too, although this was only considered small stuff compared to bigger and more expensive things that were taken across the border. I can honestly say I did my fair share of smuggling. I was not very happy about it but I did do it and this is how it happened.

As I mentioned before. My grandmother had a shop in which she sold greengrocery, confectionery, grocery, hardware and cigarettes. Cigarettes were the most popular of all and since we opened late most of the sales were at night: Woodbine, they came in a pack of five and were cheap. Sweet Afton was in packs of twenty and Players in packs of tens and twenties and then there were Afton Major. All these were much cheaper to buy in the South, so most shopkeepers bought them there and sold them a bit cheaper and still had a little bit of profit. Of course you could not display these cigarettes openly so they were usually kept hidden and when a customer wished to buy a packet, they asked for the brand they wanted calling them the "cheap ones".

The various hiding places of these cigarettes had to change frequently because at any time, morning noon or night, the Northern customs car could stop outside the shop and four or five officers would surround the house. They would search every room in the house looking for smuggled cigarettes and it was nerve wrecking as a young girl working in the shop knowing that at any time they could come. My heart did double beats and thumps and was in my mouth more times than I can remember but it was exciting as well as frightening watching the customs going around looking for the cigarettes. A

Chapter 2 - Smuggler

professional hide and seek. They were hot, very hot at times, and then cold, then hot, very hot, so hot they nearly found them, and I was standing, heart in my mouth and shaking, trying not to look scared and watching all the other members of the family who like me were hoping the contraband would not be found. Then they would just go. The funny part of the whole search was that the customs officers would overlook the simplest place of all, and that, most of the time, was where they could have found the cigarettes. My granny had some brilliant hiding places.

My granny's house was quite big. There was a long hallway and at the end of this were the stairs. Upstairs there was a long landing at the end of which was a window overlooking The Square, which, in my childhood and teenage years, was to me something to be very proud of. The landing window had a very broad windowsill that held potted plants. It had to be dusted and cleaned. I hated doing it as every plant had to be put back carefully in its right position. There was always great care taken to keep that window clean and the sill dusted because the window sill lifted up to reveal a two foot drop to the bottom, and this was where our supply of cigarettes was stored. Every day at different times a small supply of each brand would be taken out for sale that day. It was a great honour to be allowed to do this very important job, as it had to be done in such a way that would not draw too much attention from outside. These cigarettes had to be put in various hiding places throughout the house but hiding places also had to be convenient for when customers needed fresh supplies. We had a pendulum clock, or as it was called 'a Wag of the Wall Clock' in the living room. The back of it opened and held a few packets along with an old churn in the back kitchen and underneath the cushions of an armchair, which during the day we were not allowed to sit on. The money drawer in the shop had a false flap and cigarettes were placed underneath that as well. But the best of all was an old shopping bag, which held clothes pegs and hung on the handle of the back door.

One day my mother had just come in to Granny's and about five minutes later there was a raid on the house. The famous shout rang out, "Customs!" and at that Mammy grabbed the bag from the back door and ran to the yard and started taking in the clothes, which had been washed and hung out to dry early in the morning, putting the pegs in the bag which contained a large quantity of cigarettes that day. The house was searched but nothing was found and so the customs went away. The bag on the back door proved to be the best hiding place of all. They were exciting days. A professional hide and seek game but there was a very heavy fine and court case if anything was found on the premises. We always managed to escape getting caught. The cigarettes which were sold in the shop were bought in the south and were brought into the North or shall I say smuggled because my uncle lived in Carrickmacross and my granny went there to buy her supply. My other uncles had cars and indeed she went by car several times but the risk was too great. They could lose their car if caught, plus a big fine and even a jail sentence. So Granny went by bus. At Culloville there were two customs huts, one in the North and the other in the South. There was a very large shop on the southern side of the border locally known as "The Store" and twice a week a bus would come from Carrick to the store and pick up people who were going shopping. My granny went on that bus on Saturdays and until the day I die I will always remember my very first trip on that bus as a young child.

I travelled that road in a pony and trap with my grandparents when I was a tiny little girl and every year after I started school, six weeks of my summer holidays were spent in Carrick. My Auntie Peggy would also come in a pony and trap and take me home with her. I loved going to Carrickmacross but cars were a more popular way to travel and the bus was even better. I was getting a little older now, nine or ten, and I loved getting away with Granny, and going on the bus from Culloville was a different way altogether. On that Saturday in particular, my uncle Paddy brought Granny and I in his car and left us at the Northern customs post at Culloville. We walked across the border to the store and got the bus for Carrick. It was the same when we were coming home and we would have to walk from the store back across the border where my uncle was waiting for us, usually around seven o'clock in the evening. Just across the border on the southern side going towards the store there was a little cottage on the left hand side of the road. The lane down to the cottage was overgrown with grass and tall trees and at the end of the lane was the most fascinating little cottage surrounded by country garden flowers. The old lady who lived there on her own was a very good friend of my granny. Sometimes if we were early for the bus we would call in and she would give us a cup of tea and some of her freshly baked bread. I can still smell it to this very day. She was a lovely wee person, wee because she was small in size, but so very homely and kind.

As a child my long blond hair was always kept nice. My grandfather would never allow my hair to be cut and indeed many a row occurred when just a trim was suggested. However it was washed twice a week with Stay Blond shampoo and a squeeze of lemon was put in the water to rinse it and keep it nice and shiny. But now, coming near ten years old, I was beginning to have an interest in clothes, nice dresses and shoes. That Saturday in Carrick was just great as I got a new dress and new shoes and I was as happy as I could be playing with my cousins and really having a great time. The whole day was brilliant and at around five thirty I was called in to have my tea and then get ready for going home. My Auntie Peggy was nice. I liked her very much and as I had always spent my holidays with her in the summer I was very much at ease in her house and I knew my way around every room. She told me after tea that Granny was upstairs in their bedroom and that I was to go up, which I did. On entering the room I could see the bed was covered with packets of cigarettes, Players, Sweet Afton and Afton Major etc. I just stared. Granny was opening large oblong packs and putting them singly on the bed. I thought looking at her that she appeared somewhat different and seemed to have gained weight in the few hours since I had last seen her. I had been out all day playing and riding the horses with my cousins in the fields at the back of the house. Then to my amazement, she produced a large pair of flannelette knickers. As far as I knew these knickers were the kind that old women wore but they were new and had very tight elastic around the waist and legs. I thought my granny had gone mad. Why in the world would she buy me a pair of knickers like these? It brought back to my mind one day in particular when a group of us children were coming home from school with the usual messing around and finding something to laugh at. That day we did find something, and it was these various garments hanging on clotheslines that made us laugh our heads off at the size and shape of the knickers that were hanging beside large brassieres. We wondered how any one could be so big as to fill both of them and now here I was being handed a pair of these old ladies pink knickers and told to put them on over my own.

Well with sheer disgust I took them and while I was putting them on I glanced over at my Auntie Peggy who was trying to hide the smile on her face because she knew me very well. This was now a different scene from earlier in the day when with my cousins out the back, we were on the horses, pretending to be in a circus and all going to be film stars with lovely clothes and become famous and do all the things children do when playing make-believe. Now here I was putting on these awful bloomers that were four sizes too big and flopping around me, again my thoughts flashed back in those few minutes to my days as a very little girl living on The Square when I used to go down to a pub in North Street, a very famous pub owned by a prominent person in Crossmaglen.

At the time when I would visit it was the father of this person who was there. A cordial old man. I suppose he was not really old but at my age then, all big people were old and I will remember him always with great affection. His daughter Lily had recently come to live with him because he had been ill and was recovering. It was her I went to see and my visits became more and more frequent and my memories of her will always stay with me, as she was the nicest person any one could ever hope to meet. That lovely lady would bring me upstairs to her room and dress me in long dresses with necklaces and earrings and around my shoulders she would wrap a feather boa and then give me her high heel shoes to put on. Lastly, she would tie my hair on top of my head with the most beautiful diamond comb and then send me home to show off my style. I thought to myself, 'I wonder what she'd think of my flannelette knickers?' The dressing up would become really serious when her brother and his wife and children would come home on holidays from England. My playmates then would be her nieces and we all got the same treatment we were made beautiful and totally sophisticated. Her niece, and my playmate, while she was on holiday in Crossmaglen, grew up in England and entered politics and became a Labour MP (Clare Short.) That lovely lady in her gentle way gave me a sense of dress that whenever I get ready to go out I still ask myself if she would approve.

Back to the job in hand. My granny packed the pink knickers with packets of cigarettes and in a few minutes I went from a skinny little girl to a fat looking teenager who waddled as she walked. Over this went a plastic raincoat and the two people who boarded the bus in Carrick looked very different from the two that came off it a few hours earlier. Granny looked like she was about to go into labour, with her chubby granddaughter wobbling behind her. When we got to Culloville my uncle would be waiting to pick us up, but if there were any sign of customs around we would go to Granny's friend's house and leave the cigarettes there and go back later. I made this journey on two more occasions and all the bribes of new clothes and shoes could not get me to go on that run to Carrick ever again. So there it is. I did my share of smuggling as did a lot of people in South Armagh, encouraged by none other than my dear old granny! The cigarettes? They were fine, sealed in cellophane paper. Is it any wonder I never smoked and that I cannot stand cigarettes!

From an early age I always wanted to be a hair stylist and do hairdressing but my grandmother had other plans for me. Quinn's of the Milestone in Newry was the place to be, a wholesale and retail business (a supermarket giant for its time, on Hill Street where Dunne's Stores is currently located) If you got into Quinn's to serve your time, as it was called then, you were given training and experience in the grocery business and were sure of employment. There was a long waiting list of young boys and girls waiting for the chance to get an interview and if you were lucky, and indeed lucky enough to know some one high up in Quinn's, you had a good chance of getting in. As my grandmother did a lot of business with them she felt there was no problem getting me in. There was no problem getting an interview and on the day of my interview as I was walking towards Quinn's I met my best friend who told me she had just been for an interview for hairdressing and had been accepted. She told me that the lady in question still needed more trainees and that I should call in. This was my dream come true. After spending one and a half years in greengrocery and confectionery I did not like it and did not want to spend the rest of my life in that type of work.

My interview was at ten o'clock in Quinn's, but instead I was being interviewed by the owner of a hairdressing salon in Hill Street, and was accepted as a trainee hairdresser and could start as soon as I paid my forty-pound fees.

This covered my three years training. There was no pay for three years but if after two years I wanted to move on as an improver I could. However, she would prefer her girls to stay three years and become qualified hairstylists. My problem was how do I explain this to Granny and what about the forty pounds fees? Money was scarce, and then no wages for three years! At least in Quinn's you got your bus fare and a little bit more. The bus fare was twenty-one shillings for a weekly ticket. In today's money one pound and five pence. Quinn's paid thirty shillings and at least if I was there I could pay my bus fare and still have money to buy my lunch, but I thought to myself I would work something out later on. When I got home that evening my grandmother asked how I got on with my interview. I smiled and said I got the job and could start on Monday, but I didn't tell her it was a hairdressing job.

I thought I would leave it until she was in a good mood. Granny was very seldom in a bad mood but she had her days when she had worries. My grandfather was seven years dead by now and she was left with a family of eight girls and four boys and a business to carry on so she had plenty to worry her. She knew I did not go to Quinn's that day but did not say anything. A neighbour of ours had been working in Quinn's for a number of years and unknown to me she had already arranged a lift for me when I started my work. He had his own car and so he brought people into work with him. They paid a small amount of money towards petrol and it was still cheaper than going on the bus, and more convenient as you did not have to leave so early in the morning and you got home earlier in the evening. However, she had told him to look out for me on the day of the interview and to ring her and tell her how I got on. I had a lot of explaining to do but in the end her answer was that she hoped I would always be so determined about what I wanted and to go for it.

I started work the following Monday in Newry. If the bus got in early, most people went to the cathedral to say a prayer, so like every one else I went there and did what all the others did. The girls would bless themselves and kneel down along the back seat and the young men would stand at the back around the holy water font. I learned afterwards that this served three purposes. First the prayer was a quick one, and then they watched the girl's faces as they blessed themselves and when the girls knelt down the boys could see their legs. That was the explanation I got when I asked why they always stayed at the back of the church.

On my way out of the cathedral that Monday morning as I walked towards the door a group of young men were standing there. Pat Toner was one of them. I had not seen him for some time and little did I realise then that very soon I would see him again.

In those days when starting to train as a hairdresser you began with cleaning, sweeping floors and doing general housework and running errands. In fact the apprentice did most jobs that needed to be done. One thing I will always remember was the stairs. The salon was on the second floor beside the offices of the local newspaper "The Frontier Sentinel". These offices were always very busy on Mondays as people, especially country people placed advertisements on that day for the mid week paper.

Monday was also the day that the two flights of stairs had to be brushed down first and then washed and the apprentice hairdressers did the stairs. We got six shillings (30 pence in today's money) for washing the stairs and as we did not get any wages, we were delighted to get those few shillings that could buy a necklace and a pair of earrings or make-up or perfume. Not all the girls did the stairs. The nice girls would not get themselves dirty. If you did the stairs on your own you got the six shillings but if two girls worked together then the money was split. Many of us took turns to do them every other week, as we needed the money. We wore a big long black apron and with a bucket of water and a floor cloth started the work. Not a nice job. Worse still, as soon as you would start to wash the stairs people would start arriving to place an advertisement in the paper and what should have taken about half an hour, would take from early morning to near lunch time because we would have to stop to let people past and stop again as they were coming down from the office after placing the advert in the paper. It was fun but also a bit embarrassing. Especially if someone from Crossmaglen came up or some nice looking young fellow came past and me on my knees wearing a long black apron and a cloth in my hand and a bucket of dirty water. Not a very attractive sight. I also had to light the fire and we were taught to use newspapers, as there were plenty of them next door. Our manageress was a lady of Scottish decent and she would not waste a thing. She taught us how to twist the paper and criss-cross it and place it in rows in the grate, layer upon layer, and when there was a good few layers of paper the coal went on. It never failed and I still light my fires the same way.

On that first day at work the tea break was at eleven o'clock and my next task was to go for milk across the road to the Florentine Café. I went downstairs feeling really good in my nice white coat, which was my uniform. As I crossed the road a van slowed down and beeped the horn. Not being used to the town I jumped and ran quickly across the road. As I turned around to look, my face by now a brilliant red, it was none other than Pat Toner driving a Quinn's of the Milestone van. That was my second encounter of the day. I saw him again at lunchtime and then again as I was going to get the bus. Pat was very much involved with Gaelic football in those years and as he played with Co. Armagh Minor Team he did a lot of training and playing.

Dances were on all over the place and there were great bands on the go. This was the era of the Showbands and people followed the particular band they liked and it did not matter how far away they were playing. The next few years were spent at work, football and dancing. The Clippertones showband was becoming very popular with the crowds and were in great demand and Pat and I were becoming very popular with the Clippertones but for a completely different reason. A friend of Pat's who worked in The Milestone had a girl friend that was a member of the Clippertones and as the band had become so popular they travelled far and wide to play at dances. Carnivals were also becoming popular. Held for a week or ten days from a Sunday to the following Sunday or from Friday to the following Friday or Sunday. A large marquee was erected, usually on the outskirts of a town or village and only top bands were invited to these venues. Of course this was a great attraction and dancers would think nothing of driving any distance to attend.

One of the largest carnivals was held at Fords Cross, which is about four miles outside Crossmaglen. It was the ideal venue for dancers from both the North and South and you were sure to hear the very best of musicians and singers and to dance to some of the best bands of the showband age. The dances would go on until two in the morning and after the band stopped playing people would stay around for ages because the atmosphere was so good. To walk home on those lovely summer nights was a pleasure. There was no trouble and everyone talked about the great night's craic and the great bands. They were very happy times then and very quiet and peaceful. Pat's friend did not dance and as his girlfriend played in the band there was very little chance of them being together. Dances usually started at nine o' clock and went on until two a.m. with a break of ten to fifteen minutes in which two members of the band would play so that the others could have a break. Pat and I did not earn a lot of money, so to go to dances we got a lift and paid so much towards the petrol. As we all got out of the car the driver gave us a time to be back and if you were not back at the time arranged the driver would leave without you. Not all the passengers had girlfriends or boyfriends with them so at the dance if any of the boys or the girls clicked, I think they call it 'shifting' nowadays, they did not have much time to do any courting unless they left the hall a short time before the last dance was called.

Now by leaving the hall too early you got a bad reputation so it was always better to give yourself enough time to have a court, a few kisses or whatever and be back to the car at the time arranged by the driver.

This was a difficult thing to do because you would get held up in the crowd coming out from the hall. The boy would have to leave the girl at the car or bus or whatever way she was travelling, and then run quickly to be in time for his own lift. We would be sitting in the car waiting for the rest to come, which suited us fine as we were travelling together anyway. Then the poor bloke who rushed back to get his lift would arrive panting and sweating. Then the slagging would start. 'What was he at that had him all hot and bothered and so on?'

Then there were the people who did not click and would not want to wait for anyone. They would tell the driver to go on and leave the late ones to walk home. Many a young man did have to walk home and others would go home in a different car but in those days you could walk home and come to no harm. We did walk miles ourselves and sang all along the road and none of the crowd we went around with ever came to any harm. That was our South Armagh in those days and as far as we were concerned they were happy carefree days. During these times garages would hire out cars for the weekend, costing around five pounds. Considering that in the Fifties one week's wages for a young person was five pounds, this was something very few of us could afford. Some young couples shared the expenses, which covered the cost of the car and the petrol. The car was hired from Friday evening and returned on Monday morning. Pat Toner could drive but did not have the money. His friend could not drive but he offered to put up the money to hire a car at the weekends. We went everywhere the Clippertones played and Pat's friend was with us for one reason only. To be there when the band stopped playing. When you have a girlfriend who plays in a very successful showband it is very difficult to get to see each other, especially at weekends. That was how it was and without them we would never have been able to travel so much.

Chapter 3
EMIGRATION

We were returning from a dance in Drogheda, in the south of Ireland, on a Sunday about three in the morning and had just come through Dundalk heading towards Carrickarnon where there were customs stations at the border North and South. We were going along pretty fast when all of a sudden a man wearing dark clothes and a beret came onto the road in front of us, put his hand up, and stopped us. We stopped and the next thing about one hundred and fifty yards away from us there was an explosion and up went the frontier post on the northern side of the border. There were pieces of burning wood flying all over the place with smoke all over the road. Next thing the same man comes and waves us on. We were petrified and did not know what to do. We wanted to turn back but he kept waving us on and we could hardly see the road because of the black smoke but he made us keep going. We had to pick our way through pieces of burning wood and smoke and when we eventually got through, Pat drove the car as fast as he could down the road to Newry. We were the only car on the road at that time and if we had been stopped no one would believe that we were people just travelling home from a dance and were caught up in this explosion.

That was in the Fifties, during the border IRA campaign, when they were blowing up the customs posts, transformers and making raids on the police barracks. It was all starting to happen then. We had heard of more and more incidents and we were slowly starting to lose our carefree approach to life and not anxious to travel too far away not knowing what might be encountered. What was the purpose of blowing up transformers and leaving people in darkness without electricity for days on end? I could never understand it.

Pat's friend bought a car shortly after that incident and learned to drive and a short time after that Pat bought a car and we went our separate ways. We still followed the Clippertones though.

In 1959 Pat decided to go to England after a friend he went around with had gone to Middlesborough and told him of all the work that was there and how great the money was. It was difficult to get work at home. I know Pat had a job in Quinn's but the wages never changed because if you were not happy with your job, there was always someone else who needed a job. If you made a complaint you were told you could go. The day he left to go to England Pat got the train from the station at Edward Street in Newry. There was a little café at the bottom of Monaghan Street across from the railway station and we met there for a cup of tea. He took the train to Belfast and the boat to England. I was heartbroken to say goodbye, as I did not know when I would see him again. Or ever see him again. After Pat left I continued to work in Newry to complete my training as a hairdresser.

During that time I made friends with a girl in work from Mayobridge who would come home with me some weekends and stay over. It was during one of these weekends that she met her future husband from Crossmaglen. They had a whirlwind romance, got married and went to live in England. In one of her letters to me she extended an invitation that if I ever wanted to go to England I was welcome to come and stay with her and her husband.

When Pat came home for the Easter holidays and as I had thought about going to England, I decided to go back with him and his friend Sean. My family were not in favour of me going but as usual I managed to persuade them. It was good to have the company although we were not going to the same place. They were going to Middlesborough and I was going to Preston in Lancashire.

We kept in touch by letters and telephone and decided we would get engaged on Pat's birthday and we would get married the following year. We got married in July 1961. Pat had moved to Preston previously and so we set up home there. Home was a bed-sit. One large room where I had lived before getting married and so we stayed there to save money to buy a house. I continued to work at hairdressing. Pat got a job in Courtaulds, a rayon factory that made fabrics. He worked with all nationalities. Steve was Hungarian, Mike was English, Gill was from the Isle of Man, Jock was of course Scottish. We never did find out his right name but that was what we knew him as. Then there were others who had come from Australia. They all got on great together. We bought our house and about six months later our first baby was born in Preston Royal Infirmary. A boy, and we were very proud of him. We called him Patrick after his Dad.

Each year we came home for two weeks in the summer and it was great to meet all our friends. We found it very hard to go back, and each year it got worse. We did not like England but the work was there and so we had to go back. I was expecting our second child and the baby was due in January. In England at that time if you had your first baby normal, with no complications, the second baby was to be born at home. You were issued with the names and addresses and phone numbers of the midwives to call. There were three that covered the area we lived in and when it was near time for the baby to be born Pat would always ask me if I felt all right because he worked shift work. On the particular night he was working from 10 pm until 6 am. Before he left I was fine so he was happy enough to go. I did have my grandmother staying with me as she had travelled over just to be there if she was needed.

Pat was not gone an hour when I went into labour. We did not have much contact with our neighbours for in England people were too busy going and coming from work to be bothered with neighbours. So it was in those days. There was a shop across the road from us that belonged to a Tommy Thompson, who was a famous soccer player for Preston North End. I always did his wife's hair and I knew them to speak to. She told me to knock her door if I needed to make a phone call, as we did not have a phone in our house then. Across the back alley was a shop where I did my shopping each week, but it had just changed hands and I was not very familiar with the new owners. I went into labour and Granny and I went across the road to knock Mrs Thompson's door but there was no answer. As it was too far away to go to the telephone kiosk, there was no way I would be able to go as the pains were getting worse. We decided to go across the back alleyway and call on the new people in the shop for help and use their telephone. They were absolutely marvellous. The wife was a retired nurse and she brought me back home. By this time I was well in labour. Her husband arrived at the door about fifteen minutes later and he was furious, but not with us. He explained what was happening. When he rang the first number I had given him the midwife was out on a call. When he rang the second number the midwife was there but was off duty and when he rang the third number, the midwife, was gone on a call. So he rang back to the second midwife explained the situation but she said she was off duty and was not coming. Then he rang an ambulance, but because I was not booked in to have my baby in hospital they would not come either. That was England in 1964. We finally managed to get the superintendent over all the midwives and when she heard what had happened she came herself at 3.30 am, and our daughter Sheila was born at a 3.45 am. Fifteen minutes later. Pat arrived home at the usual time, 6.30 am, to find his new baby daughter asleep in her cot and the midwife waiting for him to leave her home. On leaving she told us that another nurse would arrive at around 9 am and we were to have the baby bottles boiled and everything ready for her. There were no sterilizers then, so everything had to be boiled.

Pat had just arrived back when there was a knock on the door. He opened it and a nurse came in and pushed past him. She came straight upstairs, never looked at me and went straight to the baby. Next thing she took the baby out of her cot and literally threw her on the bed. I yelled at her to stop being so rough but she continued to carry on. She never spoke to me at all. Then Pat came into the room and I started to tell him what she had done. She said that he had been abusive to one of her colleagues and that they were doing something about it. Next thing the door got an unmerciful bang and Pat ran down the stairs but before he got down, Granny had opened the door and as he was near the bottom step he came face to face with what you could only describe as the greatest bully ever. This bully arrived in the room and verbally attacked Pat! How dare he speak to one of her nurses in the way he did. Remember, I was after giving birth a few hours before. When Pat explained to her that he was at work and was not there at the time and that only for the kindness of a neighbour, things could have been much worse. Without changing her tone to Pat she then demanded to know the name of this man so she could have him reprimanded. Pat refused, saying how grateful he was that this person was there at the time and also told her that had he himself been there, he would have been up to her house and brought her down by the scruff of the neck. She left with the words "You Irish. You want it all, cream as well as the milk".

That was how our daughter came into this world. It was also the first of many encounters that her father was to have with 'Authorities' over the coming years.

We found out later that the man who had helped us that night asked her on the telephone to get down from her high horse for Gods sake and come and help this woman who was about to give birth. We found out as well that he and his wife lost a baby in similar circumstances and that she left nursing because of it. We were more determined than ever to return to Ireland but in the meantime we needed a house with a garden.

We sat one night and talked about home, and about all the nice houses the council were building and all those journeys home and then back to England again. I will never forget that boat journey. Packed full of people with sad faces, going back to a foreign land. Knowing in their hearts and souls that they did not want to go but that they had to because there was no work in Ireland. Then on arrival, there was the dreaded train journey and the cold and miserable platform where you stood, tired and heartbroken. In those days we sat up all night on the boat because it was so expensive to book a cabin. By the time we arrived at the station we were exhausted and we were only crossing to England! How those poor people, who went to America to begin a new life, must have felt, I can only wonder.

There was always a feeling of wanting to go back home. I came from a large family, six boys and six girls, and I missed them very much and more so when our children were born. I used to sit nights at home in Preston when Pat was working the night shift and think of them all at home in my mother's and the great fun and jokes and pranks they would get up to and I very much wanted to go home. I had a dream one night and in that dream Pat had built a car. This car was able to go on land and sea and we travelled home for the weekend to Crossmaglen and Forkhill. When we arrived, everywhere around us was so bright and green and all the people we met were smiling and happy, and there was a great feeling of peace and contentment. Then I woke up. I knew we were not able to go back just yet, but with that dream in my heart we waited, and eventually we were able to come home.

We came home in April 1964 and lived with Pat's mother in Forkhill. Our son was coming on two years old and our daughter was three months old. We needed a house and as the local council were responsible for housing in those days, the procedure was to put your name down on a waiting list with the council. There was a very long waiting list but we did not mind where we got a house as long as we got one. After about three months waiting we got one of the new houses that had just been finished at Creggan, just a few miles outside Crossmaglen.

Pat had no job but we managed to keep going on what little savings we had. He played football for Forkhill before going to England and was well known in the county. I remember on one of the telegrams we received on our wedding day was the message "Good luck, and God bless you. Who will they play for, Stars or Rangers?" Forkhill football club, before Pat went to England, was known as the Stars and Crossmaglen of course was known as the Rangers and until this day still are. It was no surprise then when he was approached to play football for Crossmaglen, he declined, because if Pat was going to play football again it would be for Forkhill, his own home team. Pat did get involved with the youth club in Crossmaglen and did play football with Crossmaglen Rangers, but during a match, he sustained an injury [cracked ribs] from a tackle on the field and had to stop playing, but later with the youth club he was very active with the young people. There was a young policeman, a sergeant stationed in Crossmaglen RUC barracks. He was a very athletic young man and very much involved with the youth club at the time. It was like that in Crossmaglen in those days. Pat also joined the Forrester's in Forkhill where his father had been a member for years. I had been doing a Novena to St Therese, a little prayer that I said for nine days. Usually you will get your prayer answered at the end of the nine days. My request was the hope that Pat would get a job. We were at home almost a year and it was difficult to make ends meet. He had applied for a job with Cumiskey's, a department store in Dundalk which sold household goods, carpets, furniture, and musical instruments and we were both delighted when they contacted him and said he had got the job. That was in 1965 and he was with them for fourteen years working as a salesman throughout Co. Louth and South Armagh.

Our second son Morgan was born at home at Creggan in April 1966 on Ash Wednesday. He was born at home and in a much better way than our daughter in England. I got the best care and attention anyone could get. Before I had become pregnant with our third child I had wanted to start hairdressing in Crossmaglen. The old Belfast Bank was been renovated into units and so I applied for one but little did I realise then that the morning I opened my shop I would have a six weeks old baby at home. Anyway I managed with the help of my mother and my grandmother, but it was not easy. Our eldest child had started school and in the mornings I had to leave him at school and bring my daughter and the baby with me and Mammy or Granny would look after them. It was a lot of pressure and I must admire the young mothers today who go out to work because I know it is not easy to keep a job and look after children, a home and a husband. In the Sixties, when our children were small there were not a lot of mothers who worked. In recent years the rising cost of living has put a lot of demand on young mothers to get jobs to be able to support their family, and I think that these days children expect too much from their parents and put them under far too much pressure. Anyway, for us there came an opportunity, which we thought might make things a little easier for us or for me at least.

There was a house for sale in Mullaghbawn. It was Murdock's shop. The local grocery shop and post office. After Mrs Murdock retired the house was sold and was bought by a local man who had it renovated and put it up for sale again. We bought the house in Mullaghbawn for two thousand five hundred pounds. Living here meant I could still do hairdressing and look after the children in the house without having to go out. The baby was seven months when we moved to Mullaghbawn and our eldest son transferred from school in Crossmaglen to

Mullaghbawn and our daughter started in the girls primary school. I continued to do hairdressing and Pat still had his job in Dundalk and travelled around Louth and South Armagh.

Through his work he got to know a lot of people and I got to know many through hairdressing. The curate in Mullaghbawn at that time was Father Murtagh. A great man for drama and he also loved music. In 1966 'Top Team' talent competitions were very popular where towns north and south of the border would compete against each other and this provided great entertainment. These competitions went for weeks leading to two semi finals and then an overall final. Father Murtagh was very anxious to get a local team. So one night, after Pat and I had been singing in a concert which he had organised along with the help of a friend from Dundalk, he asked us if we would start up a local talent group. We thought about it for a while and then I contacted my Auntie Minnie Clarke who was a very talented pianist. Although she was blind, this was never a problem to her. Minnie was educated as a young girl at a convent boarding school in Whitabbey in Co. Antrim. My grandfather and grandmother were determined that although she was blind she would get every opportunity to develop gifts that she had been blessed with. In her teenage years she studied music lessons in Belfast. Taught by her music teacher for the blind, Mr. Taylor, who was blind himself. She studied and read in braille, which is a system of reading with raised letters for the blind. All her exams completed, she continued her studies through The Guildhall School of Music and Drama in London and got her diploma, and qualified as a music teacher. Minnie returned to Crossmaglen and taught music at her home on The Square. She was also the organist for Crossmaglen Chapel for the rest of her life. She was ready to play for us and to give us her help and being such a talented person and a brilliant pianist we decided to give it a go.

We called a meeting and asked anyone who could sing or dance, tell stories or play musical instruments to please come to the hall with regard to starting a talent group to take part in the competitions. The talent that came forward was unbelievable. An abundance just waiting to explode. Young children, teenagers and people in their twenties and thirties. We started rehearsing and planning the different scenes which we were going to use because throughout these shows points were given for production, talent, presentation, costumes, most topical, most comical, best singer and best musician. We had been rehearsing for a few weeks and every night at those rehearsals I noticed a young man sitting at the back of the hall. He sat in the same place every night and one night I shouted down to him from the stage and asked him if there was anything he could do and perhaps take part in the show. He walked towards the stage with an electric guitar and played the "Masons Apron". This reel is usually played on a fiddle and is a very difficult piece of music to play but to perform it on an electric guitar is just phenomenal. When he finished playing everyone in the hall gathered around this talented man who was so very shy, and so very quiet. He was of course the late Bernard Heaney. I mention his name here with great pride because he joined our group that night and went on to compere every show we did and he brought great pleasure to audiences wherever we performed. We became known as The Belmont Talent Group from Mullaghbawn and with Bernard, our compere and our wonderful cast we beat the cream of those talent shows. No one was more pleased with it all than Father Murtagh, the man who planted the idea.

Our house in Mullaghbawn was quite big and as we did not need all the space we decided to start a small shop. We needed to do some alterations to the side of the house and make a separate entrance involving breaking the wall to make a door into the shop from the side of the house. There was a garden at the side which was entered by a small gate with two granite pillars each side which had to be taken away to make an entrance into the shop. We got in touch with a local builder who took on the work and started at once. Rumour got around that we were starting a shop, for news like that spreads fast in the country area and as we were new people into the area this attracted a lot of interest. A few problems did arise, but we overcame them and eventually got the business going. Living in Mullaghbawn at the same time as Pat and myself was Paddy O' Hanlon, a very prominent young man who was very much involved with the Civil Rights Movement. He had returned to his native village and was working along with his colleagues in the Civil Rights Movement. Pat had great respect and admiration for Paddy O'Hanlon and it was no surprise to me when he befriended him and became involved with him and the Civil Rights Movement. They became great friends and when Paddy decided that he would contest the South Armagh seat at Stormont in 1969, Pat offered his support. In doing so he was making his own entry into politics. Paddy O'Hanlon opposed the sitting MP Eddie Richardson. It was quite an election. I had heard over many years of how elections were fought in South Armagh, but this was the father of them all. Paddy O'Hanlon won that election and now we had new blood in South Armagh and the future seemed bright. Pat was working in Dundalk and was still travelling around the South Armagh area, which was part of his job. He was still very much involved in his work with the youth club and with football. The work as a mother, a hairdresser and trying to run a business took its toll. I tried so hard to do everything well and our children did always come first and because I put so much effort into this, my professional work put a lot of pressure on me.

Hairdressing is a very demanding profession. Not only was I a stylist but also I was a sympathetic listener to many problems from my clients. I was a counsellor, not qualified of course, but I listened to many stories and problems, which any one in this profession today can identify with. Although I had many problems of my own, these were never important when a mother or grandmother or some person had something on their minds, which they wanted to talk about. I listened and gave advice where and when I could. I can honestly say that I have heard some very sad stories and listened to some of the most tragic and heart rendering problems. It was unbelievable. This taught me through the years that when you meet people and talk to them that behind all those smiles and being pleasant, a lot of times there is a lot of heartache.

When we were living at Creggan and I was working as a hairdresser in Crossmaglen, our second son was just a baby so both my mother and grandmother helped in turn to look after him for me. Our other two children were at primary school and they would come after school to either house depending on which person was looking after the baby on that day. I had a lovely little nephew, Brendan Rushe who was my Auntie Janie's son. Brendan was ten years old and every day after school he would come to play with the baby. He loved to take him for a walk and would wheel the baby in the pram up and down the street all evening and like any young boy he would be delighted with a small reward for his help. As with all children this would be some money to buy sweets. After we moved to Mullaghbawn I would take Tuesday off work and go to Crossmaglen with the baby while the other children were at school. I could get the Crossmaglen bus, which left Newry at 9.15 via Mullaghbawn and stopping at O'Hanlon's pub, which was just down the road from our house. That bus got to Cross at 10 o'clock. I could spend some time at home, do some shopping and get the 2 pm bus leaving Cross to get me home to Mullaghbawn in time for the two older children coming in from school. Another reason for my going to Crossmaglen on Tuesdays was that my family allowance book had not yet been transferred. I had listened so often to some of my clients telling me how they could leave their money lying for a couple of months. Well maybe I was a bad manager at the time or maybe I just needed an excuse to go to Crossmaglen. Either way, those Tuesdays were a very important journey for me. On one of those Tuesdays while I was in Crossmaglen, the same young Brendan Rushe offered to go to the Post Office to collect my money for me. When a child goes an errand most of us will give them a small amount of money but on that particular day I had no small change when the little boy came back, and as the bus was ready to leave, I said to him that next Tuesday when I came back I would make it up to him. He was a beautiful child and I will always remember those big brown eyes looking up at me. He said it was all right and that he didn't want anything. I bade him goodbye and got the bus home.

On Thursday morning at eight o'clock we got a phone call. It was another aunt who rang to tell us that Brendan had drowned in Lough Ross, outside Crossmaglen, on the Wednesday evening. He had gone with his brothers and pals. They were fishing and that's when the accident happened. For the rest of my life I will carry this awful feeling. Why didn't I get some change? Why didn't I tell my mother to give him some money for me? I know he gladly went the errand for me, not expecting any payment in return, but it just seemed so sad to think I would never get the chance to make up to him for all the help he had given to us. How many of us today will feel in some way that we never did enough for someone. Pat went to work I remember, after the two older children went to school. I put the baby in his pram and put him outside the front door and I went and sat on the front step alongside the pram. I couldn't go back into the house. I felt so overwhelmed with my emotions. I felt so alone and so helpless, I couldn't work and I just cried and cried. With the pressure of work and with this tragedy it had all become too much. I rang Pat at work and he came home and we collected the children from school. Pat brought me straight to my mother's and I never went back to our house in Mullaghbawn.

Chapter 4
INTO POLITICS

Since our return home from England Pat always said that eventually he would like to live in Forkhill. When we bought the house in Mullaghbawn, I remember saying to him "You are getting nearer to Forkhill". He laughed and said "Not really Christine". I did not realize then that he would get his wish but I knew that was where he really wanted to be and with the way things turned out for us as a family, and because I did not want to return to our house in Mullaghbawn we put our house up for sale. Pat approached our local councillor about getting a house in Forkhill but there were no houses available at that time. The councillor told him that as soon as one became available we would get it. We sold our house in Mullaghbawn and in a few months time we got a house in Forkhill. We settled in Forkhill and Pat continued to work in Dundalk.

Pat was still involved with Paddy O'Hanlon and by this time the SDLP party was progressing and meetings were held in Newry. They both travelled together to those meetings. Pat had by now become a member of the SDLP party and Paddy O'Hanlon was chief whip of the SDLP and so it was time to start a local branch of the party in South Armagh. The areas to cover were Newtownhamilton, Camlough, Lislea, Crossmaglen, Mullaghbawn and Forkhill. With preparation made, the inaugural meeting was held in Mullaghbawn Hall. There were fifteen people in the hall that night including a young curate (Priest) from Camlough as well as Pat and Paddy. The meeting had just begun when a group of people, demonstrating, burst in the door of the hall and in a very aggressive manner started to verbally attack the people who were taking part. Their language was extremely abusive and at one stage only for the intervention of the curate from Camlough there would have been some very nasty scenes. Indeed these people who were a republican element were intent on not allowing the SDLP to start a branch in South Armagh. But neither Pat Toner nor Paddy O'Hanlon were easy people to frighten. The branch wasn't formed that night but two weeks later it was with an additional ten more members, making a total of twenty-five members from throughout the South Armagh area. This was the beginning of SDLP in South Armagh.

Thursday was Pat's day off and we usually went into Newry. I got ready and Pat said he was going via Mullaghbawn as he was giving Paddy O' Hanlon a lift. We collected him and he said "By the way Christine, have you heard who the SDLP candidate is for area E in the coming elections?" I was so preoccupied with getting the new house in order that I was not aware of the forthcoming elections. I was not very much interested in politics at the time but I was so very concerned about the future, as were many people, after the awful killings on Bloody Sunday in Derry on the 30th January 1972 when the Parachute Regiment of the British Army shot dead thirteen men following a peaceful civil rights march from the Creggan Estate in Derry. Seventeen others were injured in that incident which lasted over half an hour. My mind went back to that day. I remember it very well. We were in our house in Forkhill a short time and we were still trying to get some decorating done. We had bought carpet for the children's bedroom and as it was Sunday, and Pat was at home, he said he would put it down for me. We had the radio on and the programme was interrupted for a news bulletin and that was how we heard about what had happened. The carpet didn't seem important after hearing the news of the killings. It was so terrible we could not think of doing any work and we did nothing for the remainder of the evening but watch television and every news item until bedtime.

I did not want to show my ignorance with regard to the elections so I said to Paddy that I wasn't awfully sure. I knew that Sean Mc Creesh was a councillor as was his father before him; Mickey Mc Creesh was a councillor for many years with Newry No. 2 Council, as it was known at that time. After his father's death Sean ran for council. He was elected as a councillor and had continued in council for a number of years. There was to be a completely different scene now with the disbandment of Stormont and the suspension of local government. Reform of local government had been introduced in 1973 and the new council was to be known as Newry and Mourne District Council. It was divided into five electoral areas taking in Newry, South Armagh and South Down. Area A covered Kilkeel and Annalong; area B Rostrevor and Warrenpoint; Area C Newry town; area D Killeavy, Bessbrook and Camlough and Newtownhamilton and area E Crossmaglen, Mullaghbawn, Dromintee and Forkhill. What I did not know was that Pat had been asked to run for council as an SDLP candidate many weeks earlier. However, as his father had been ill and had died only a few weeks before nomination day, it was decided to leave things as long as possible so he could have some time with the family. The last thing on anyone's mind was the forthcoming election so on that day in the car travelling to Newry you can imagine my surprise when after Paddy's question as to my knowing who the local candidate was, he laughed and said "you're sitting beside him".

That's when I knew that Pat was going for election and he was on his way in to Newry to hand in his nomination papers. This was the beginning of what was to be for Pat, for me and our children the start of thirty years of involvement in local government. When the campaign began, our youngest child Sharina was under two years old and our eldest son was about to go to secondary school. It was a very big step to take. There was a lot of election canvassing to be done and a lot of preparation. It was all new to us and although being a member of a party brings a lot of support, it did not give any financial help for council elections so there was a lot of organisation at our own expense. In those days, with a young family, money was not easy to come by. Pat carried on with his job and most of the organising was done at night when he came home. I wasn't very happy at all about this whole intrusion in our lives but little did I know that the real intrusion in our lives had just begun. We were just starting to get settled in Forkhill and there were still a lot of things to be done but it would have to wait until after the election. But now that Pat had decided to run I would support him just as he had supported me when I needed his help. It was very difficult to get into the swing of canvassing. It was Northern Ireland's first elections for six years and the first since the change in the electoral laws, which established the principle of "One Man, One Vote".

They were the first elections in which everyone over the age of 18 had a vote and the first for nearly half a century using the Proportional Representation (PR) system of voting. The 26 new councils would have a total membership of around 500 councillors, chosen by just over one million voters. So here it was. There was no turning back. The nomination papers were in and the show was on the road. We were thrown in at the deep end and sink or swim we had to go on. Those seeking seats in the new council were mostly involved with various parties; Alliance, Unionist, Irish Labour, SDLP, Republican, Independent Republican and several Independents and among the candidates were councillors and former councillors. The new 30 strong council was scheduled to hold meetings in Newry in October. Those elected would also form a percentage of the new statutory authorities set up by the government to operate services such as health, welfare, libraries and education.

If you were 18 or over on polling day and your name was on the 1973 register, you were entitled to vote. The PR system of voting 1, 2, and 3 in order of preference looked easy but it was hard for a lot of people to understand. The young people picked it up quickly but a lot of the older generation found it very hard to understand as they were used to placing an X at the name of the person that they wished to vote for. When we were canvassing we found that this was what many could not follow easily. In a statement, the South Down and South Armagh command staff of the Provisional IRA called for a boycott of all local and government elections until every man and woman held without trial or charge were released. This of course refers to the introduction of internment in August 1971. On the 9th of August that year 342 people, all of whom were described as republican suspects were interned. One third were released within two days but many other arrests followed. We all hoped that 1973 would be a beginning to work towards a better future. A lot had happened in our country and a lot of injustice had been done and there had to be change and the right sort of change. People now had the right to go out and vote for what they wanted. The men and women who went on the march for Civil Rights had worked so hard to give us "One Man, One Vote". Canvassing started seriously two weeks before the election. The SDLP put up 5 candidates for area E in South Armagh. Owen Kelly, Jack Mc Mahon, James Mc Parland, Jim Murphy and Pat Toner. Pat's Sister Rita was very good and she offered to look after the children for us during campaigning. We had no experience of elections. Pat had canvassed for Paddy O' Hanlon and had his first taste of it then but I certainly did not. I did sit in the polling station as personating officer for Paddy O'Hanlon in Crossmaglen, for his election but never in my wildest dreams could I have imagined what was ahead of us.

I wasn't with Pat all the time but when I was, the abuse we had to endure was unbelievable. This was not from people whose door we knocked to ask for their vote. I never really realised how well known Pat was around the area he was going to represent, but then he did play football and he worked around the country and knew a lot of the farmers. I knew a lot of people too from Crossmaglen. But the nasty people were on the road and hanging around the various housing estates. They were not Crossmaglen people but they had followed us along the way as we were canvassing and stayed and shouted abuse at us everywhere we stopped. Looking back now, the local people were embarrassed. The SDLP was a new party and this was the beginning of a new era and although everyone wanted change, lurking in the shadows were those who wanted to bully and dictate, threaten and try to scare people into their way of thinking. We both knew by now that all this was not going to be easy but it was already started and so we had to go on and we did. Pat was in Ardross housing estate in Crossmaglen, canvassing door to door. He noticed a van driving slowly as he went along the houses, the occupants were shouting abuse at him. "Go home quisling, traitor. You are not wanted here." Pat carried on knocking on doors. Although some doors opened, most did not. As he was leaving one of the houses. The van pulled up along side him and the sliding door opened and a gun was pointed at him. He thought; should he dive to the ground or run, but made a decision to carry on canvassing. Finally the van drove off. A few days later Pat was canvassing on the Ballsmill Road. It was night time and as he drove along a car came up behind him and flashed its lights, Pat pulled in to allow it to pass. The car pulled in blocking him and a second car pulled in behind him. Pat got out of his car and went to the car behind. At this point he thought, "This is it, I'm going to be done". Throughout his life he would, when confronted with any type of danger retaliate by getting very angry and brave. The window on the driver's side was down. He grabbed the driver and started to shake him, saying, "I presume you are the Provos. What are you at? I am only doing what you are fighting for. Freedom for people to do as they want. All I am doing is asking for people to vote for me if they so desire". From the back seat of the car a middle aged man sitting between two young people said "Leave that man alone, he makes sense." From that night on Pat had very few problems from the republican elements. He always said he would like to know who that man was, and perhaps meet him, sometime somewhere. There were, some years later, times when Pat was confronted with danger and intimidation. On one occasion during a European election when John Hume and helpers were canvassing in Crossmaglen, there was a lot of abuse and harassment from a small number of people. Some of their behaviour was threatening and very aggressive. However, most of Crossmaglen was canvassed and covered, and so the cavalcade headed towards Creggan. Pat was driving the lead car and he was surveying, ahead of the main group. Travelling with him was Paddy O'Hanlon and our son Patrick. Coming towards Creggan Bridge Pat spotted a group of people on the Old Road at the bridge. He braked because he saw the danger, stopped the car, got out and started to walk towards the menacing group who were there to ambush John Hume and the rest of the cavalcade. When Pat started to walk towards them they started to hurl stones and other missiles at him. Most of the group were women. Very few men were involved. As Pat continued to walk towards them, our son Patrick and Paddy O'Hanlon were out of the car shouting at Pat to come back or he'd be killed. Pat continued, ducking the missiles and calling to the man, a big burly person, to come out from behind the women and face him man to man. For some unknown reason, which Pat could never understand they all skulked away down the road, and so the canvassing continued. Pat always maintained that some person in that group said, "This man is mad, let's leave him alone". I knew my husband and he would not be a person to back down to anyone, under any circumstances, regardless of any threat or intimidation. Patrick, our son, always told the story which Paddy O'Hanlon repeated many times about that day. Paddy said "We were at Creggan Bridge with stones been hurled at us and the next thing wee Toner went for them like a bull, ducking and weaving the missiles. We thought that would be the end of him and we could not believe our eyes as we watched them turn away.

The extent of the area to cover was large and so there were polling stations in Forkhill Hall and in Crossmaglen at St Patrick's Primary School. Also, in Camlough, Newtownhamilton and Newtowncloughue. Pat was scheduled to stay in Forkhill Polling Station and I was to go to Crossmaglen to be in the polling station there. Before leaving I had to cast my vote in Forkhill and after doing so Pat left me in Crossmaglen and went back to Forkhill.

I was not looking forward to this, given the fact that all through the canvassing we were seeing posters to boycott the elections and God knows we did not know what it was going to be like in Crossmaglen on polling day. Pat took me there and as we came into Crossmaglen the posters were greeting us everywhere- "Boycott the local government elections". Three days before, I had phoned into a radio station. Sean Duignan was doing a programme on the elections and we were after getting a call from a person who was very afraid to go out to vote as she had seen one poster in particular which read, "Voters are Traitors". We had seen this one ourselves and people were very scared. However, when I told Sean about this poster during our conversation on the phone-in, he couldn't believe it and I said to him "What can you say to people who ask you for advice?" He had no answer. As well as representing Pat in Crossmaglen I was to act as personating officer, believe me, this was something else.

I knew from my childhood days and teenage years about impersonating during elections. My uncles both owned cars and did a little bit of taxi driving and always at election time they had a lot of extra business. I remember some of the stories they used to tell of the antics that people got up to during election time around the South

Armagh area and especially Crossmaglen. When a candidate was going for election and had the support of the local people in the town and throughout the rural area, they made sure their man was elected even if it meant voting one, two or three times. They took great pride in doing it. To some people it was an art, to be a comedian, to dress up and look different so that they could not be recognised even by their best friends. There was always great talent around the South Armagh area. They were the best, but then they had years of experience! We all heard the stories of how some people went in to vote, came out, changed their clothes and went back in again to vote on another person's name. Indeed clothes were not all that changed; glasses and even false teeth were changed over to help alter the image of the particular individual. Indeed even gender on occasion!

There is one particular incident, which truly did happen. It was on election day which was hailed the 'father of all elections' ever in South Armagh. Two brothers lived alone for years and they always came out to vote whenever there was an election. They felt it was very important to cast their vote. Four days before the particular election, Joe lost his brother James who had suffered for some time from a chest infection. Now, in his late seventies he caught pneumonia and died. After the funeral, Joe and a few others went to a local pub to have a drink and after several drinks, Joe decided that he would vote. On leaving the polling station, he was approached by the particular candidate who expressed his gratitude on his coming to vote after laying his brother to rest. He went on to say that poor James would have loved to be able to vote. Joe said that indeed he would and the other man said that Joe could do it for him now that he was here.

Joe agreed and with a jacket to replace the topcoat, went back to the booth to vote in James' name. The anxious candidate, hoping to get as many voters in as quickly as he could, started to hurry Joe out before anyone caught on what was happening. When half way to the door Joe shouted in a loud voice "For Jasus' sake slow up! I know I just voted for James but don't rush me into the grave beside him".

There were a lot of red faces. There were always funny sides to these sorts of antics and there were always people who made election day a day out and a bit of fun. But as the years went on things changed a lot and so it became very important that it would be literally "one man, one vote" and that everyone got a fair chance. As I said, I was going to Crossmaglen to represent Pat and also to act as personating officer for himself and the party. As we arrived in Crossmaglen we were greeted with posters "Voters are Traitors" and at the corner, as we headed for the polling station two young men who were standing there started to shout abuse at us. Our car had a loud speaker on the roof and the bonnet was covered with posters, which read: "Vote SDLP 1, 2, 3, and naming the candidates in order of preference.

It was relatively quiet at the polling station. Pat left me there, as he had to return to Forkhill. I stayed there to meet people on his behalf and also to act as personating officer. It was a very difficult election. People just did not want to come out to vote. There was a lot of apathy as for weeks before the elections the public were told not to vote and quite honestly they did not know what to do. Some very brave people did come out and cast their vote but by mid afternoon the turnout was very low. I had been in constant contact with Pat throughout the day and he in turn was in contact with Newry and the other areas. Towards evening, word came to me that people in Newry had started to come out to vote and so at around six o'clock Pat came from Forkhill to Crossmaglen and we both went out in the car. Pat was driving and I was speaking on the loudspeaker, urging people to come out and cast their vote. It didn't matter whom they voted for, as long as they came out to vote.

It was during this time that we were confronted by two young men with guns. I thought it was a joke but then when I looked and saw the hatred in their eyes I knew this was no joke. It was then that I realised why Pat got involved and I decided then that I would support him all the way. I was frightened. I thought of our children, of everyone's children and I knew that we must carry on and do what we could to encourage people to come out and vote. People started to come out. Maybe it was that there were other people in other areas starting to come out, and although the turnout was bad - out of 1,500 people only about 120 voted. It got very nasty later on. By 10 pm, I had to be escorted out of Crossmaglen. Pat had left earlier to go back to Forkhill. I will always remember those very brave people who came and voted for Pat. They were brave to come past some of those people who stood and stared as each person walked into the polling station. The looks were enough to let you know what they would have liked to do.

The elections of 30 May 1973 returned 13 SDLP, 8 Unionists, 4 Alliance, 3 Independents and 2 Republican councillors. There was a lot of unrest and throughout those years leading to 1973 it was a very bad time.

Pat and I, like many families in the village of Forkhill lived in housing estates built by the Housing Executive. A lot of the older houses were built by the council years before. The one thing we all had in common was that we lived in very close proximity to the RUC barracks and its surroundings. This never caused any great problem. In fact quite a few of the married policemen lived in the housing estates with their families and they did not find any problem with the situation at all and neither did the local people. There were living quarters at the barracks for the policemen and an attached house, which was used as living accommodation for the sergeant, his wife and family. During this particular time Sergeant White was well known and liked by all the people in the community. Things in Forkhill were very different in those days as the Sergeant was on many occasions called out to solve various domestic disputes between husbands and wives. He was always helpful when he was called out regardless of the situation. The sergeant's wife and other mothers helped to run the girls' youth club, at the same time as Pat was in charge of the boys.

I remember one incident at Halloween when one of the older boys asked if they could organise a dance. This was agreed, but it would be a combined effort with both the girls' and the boys' clubs. One of the older lads knew of a good group and he would find out if they would come to the hall in Forkhill and play. It was all arranged and on the night in question the young group who came from Banbridge played extremely well and it was a brilliant night for them. It was all very well supervised. The parents helped out and everything went well until the end. Unknown to all those involved at the time a few new people had moved into the area. These were new families and the children did not attend the youth club but on the night of the dance one of the older boys of the family was there in the hall and he encouraged one of the local boys to ask the group to play the National Anthem. The young boys in the group who had only been together a short while did not know how to play the National Anthem and said they were sorry.

A stranger then produced a knife. Immediately Pat and Mrs White (the sergeant's wife), who was helping him that night, grabbed him. We never had that problem with local children in Forkhill. Thank God nobody was hurt. I remember how angry Pat was that night. The next day he made it his business to find out whom the culprit was and made it quite clear that this sort of behaviour was not wanted in Forkhill.

The youth club was great for the young people. They got to do a lot of different things and as our own children were involved we were part of whatever event was organised. Christmas '68-'69 caused great excitement because it was organised that if the weather was good we were to bring our children up the back road to the big field beside the barracks where Santa Claus was to arrive (the field later became the site for the security base). Santa arrived by helicopter and had a present for every child. We can all read the history books and find out when the army arrived, why they came in the first place but I remember that day in Forkhill when Santa arrived in a helicopter and all who brought children there that day will remember the joy on their faces forever.

Little did we know then that the young policeman who dressed up as Santa and gave up his weekend to do so, would be killed later on by a roadside bomb. Nor did we realise either that we would live with helicopters for so many years to come and that the joy and fun our children had shared that day would be replaced by some of the most awful atrocities that was to cast a shadow on them for the rest of their lives.

Chapter 5
CAUGHT BETWEEN TWO FORCES

The security forces began to build lookout posts behind the barracks and they were placed at vantage points around the different housing estates. The reason given for this was to give them a good view of the surrounding areas as most of the roads out of Forkhill lead to the border. We lived at the Fairview Estate and as the border was just over the road from there, a lookout post was erected at the top of our garden and had a clear view of the border at Dungooley. Indeed, on the spot where the new St. Oliver Plunkett Church is built, the roads leading into Dundalk could be clearly seen.

The lookout post in question was situated between our garden and that of our neighbours. About eight houses down there was another post, which gave a clear view of the Carrickasticken Road. It was the same for the people who lived on the back road as well. From then on, all had to live under surveillance, whether leaving the children to school, going shopping, going for a walk- no matter what, we were watched. There were times when it was very frustrating, as we had no privacy. We learned to live with it and indeed we learned to laugh as well.

My next-door neighbour and I had great long clotheslines in our gardens and as we all had young children, the lines were always full. Every day there was washing to be done. There were no Pampers in those days and so the Terry towelling nappies alone were enough to fill the line. However, there was other washing to be done and dried, and so we came to the hanging out of our smalls under the watchful eye of young soldiers. This had become very embarrassing and more so when a whistle or two came. Eventually, when the lookout post was erected, we all installed little lines outside our back doors so we could hang out our little bits of clothing with at least a little more privacy. In those days we did not have the luxury of tumble driers and very few of us had central heating.

We began to experience what was a more difficult situation. There were a lot of young men, who had fled from the north, following the unrest, and with the introduction of internment (imprisonment without trial) in August 1971, went on the run. There were also a lot of young men from Forkhill and surrounding areas who were involved with the Republican Movement. Fearing that they would be interned, they also went on the run. Many crossed the border into Dundalk, which is only six miles from Forkhill. Some had left a few days before internment night having been warned by the local police sergeant that internment was coming. The Sergeant knew these young men and their families and so to avoid them being interned he dropped the hint, and they got out straight away. The others left shortly afterwards. There was a lot of harassment from the soldiers in those days and young people were annoyed when they were stopped and asked for identification. They were not used to this and all at once they were told what to do and where they could and could not go. This is how a lot of their lives had changed. Some, if not all, of them would react and then things were made worse for them. When they retaliated they would get pushed about or, worse still, get beaten up. This was very hard to take, but there were even worse things to come.

Pat was a founder member of Slieve Gullion Credit Union and they, like the Irish National Foresters, had an annual dinner dance in the Ballymascanlon Hotel. This was always something to look forward to and as we did not get out much in those days, all or most of the people around the village got tickets and enjoyed the night out. There was always a lovely meal, a good band and a great night's dancing. On one of these occasions held on a Friday night, my young brother came to baby-sit for us. We went to the Ballymac Hotel and it was a great night and we came home in good form. The next morning I called my brother to get the bus leaving Forkhill for Newry at 8.30 am. He was working and had to be in for 9 am. After he left, I cleared out the fire and set it and went to put the ashes in the bin in the back yard.

As I put the lid back on the bin I heard this unmerciful rat, a, tat

tat! I stood for a moment and the same noise again only slightly louder. Next thing I heard a soldier shouting at me from the look out post at the top of the garden to get down on the ground. I didn't realise what was happening and ran into the kitchen. After two more of the same noises there was quiet. Later on we found out that the shots had come from the Dungooley direction and that some men were seen driving off in a car. There weren't many houses on the road from Forkhill to Dungooley in those days and from the hill at Dungooley just over the border from Forkhill there was a clear view of the look out posts, which were at the top of our garden.

This was to become a regular occurrence on most Saturday mornings. With Pat working in Dundalk, I would go there to do my shopping and every Saturday he would come home at lunchtime and collect the children and myself and bring us to Dundalk. The novelty of those trips for the children was to get a ride in the van. Pat had a company van, which he used at work and it was this van he used to bring the children and myself to Dundalk. The children loved the high van and all would sit in the back on the way to Dundalk. One particular Saturday one of the children was ill and we did not go on our usual trip to Dundalk. Later on in the afternoon one of our older children was out on his bike with friends and came back and told me that he saw Daddy's car at Dungooley, which is on the border in County Louth. I thought this was strange for I knew that if Pat was in the area at all he would call. When he came home I was telling him about what our child had said but he didn't comment at all. I said nothing more but much later I found out what had happened. As I stated before, a lot of local lads who were involved in the Republican Movement were on the run, living in Dundalk. These lads had accommodation in Dundalk. They came from good families and were young and maybe they all wanted to be part of the new surge of Republicanism, I personally don't quite know what they wanted. Whatever it was, they believed in what they were doing, but looking back now I think some of them soon realised not to become too deeply involved. Living in Dundalk at that time were two well-known leading republicans from Belfast and they had a great influence on these young people. Pat worked in a furniture shop, which sold new and second hand furniture. In most cases people would give in their old furniture in part exchange for new and Pat had access to a lot of second hand furniture. He gave these young men beds to sleep on and helped them in any way he could. Some of them had accommodation above the shop he worked in and so they knew he was there every day. On a few occasions he was asked for his car as it was parked outside the shop. He did not like refusing them especially when they would use the excuse that they were meeting their mother or other members of the family outside Dundalk. Later we found out that our car was at Dungooly on the border in County Louth about three quarters of a mile from Forkhill, on two occasions when shots were taken at the look-out posts and army patrols in Forkhill.

There was never any thought at that time that local people's lives were in danger. I think it was a bit of fun to them, scaring the wits out of the soldiers. Then one day when the soldiers were out on patrol they fired back and a local lad was injured. Although not badly, it was enough to land him in hospital in Dundalk, and later Dublin. His parents couldn't find out anything about him. We knew them and Pat contacted Paddy O' Hanlon and very soon we were able to let his parents know he was all right and in no danger. The fun and games were over after that incident. Months later during the summer holidays I had my sister's daughter staying with us. She was playing at the top of the garden with our own children in the late afternoon and suddenly there was a burst of gunfire. This time it was stronger and more continuous than any of the other shots. The children were at the top of the garden and I ran out and yelled at them to lie down. I screamed at them to get down on the grass and to crawl on their bellies until they got to the back door.

At this time the soldier in the look-out post was shouting at them also and they were terrified. By the time they got to the house they were hysterical and so was I. I took the clay and grass from under their fingernails. The attack lasted half an hour but it seemed like hours. That little girl, who is married now and has her own children, was on her holidays in Forkhill and I'm sure she tells them often about her experience. She never came back to stay. That was the beginning of the serious attacks. From then on, patrols in the areas were fired on at every opportunity. We did not know when there might be an attack. The children were told to be careful and not to go too far away from the house and definitely not over the fields.

How does a young child understand? After all, from the time they learn to walk, their first great ambition is to get out on the road and follow the older children down the street, to get out of the garden prison that has protected them from danger. To cross the gate was the first big move and it always took time to master. Every child in Fairview had different ways of doing so and we watched them all. It was part of growing up and we had such a lovely village and countryside that it was only right it should be explored. Later on we would learn how the innocence of climbing a gate would lead to a terrible tragedy.

Now all the children in the village were to be deprived of their freedom. We as adults did not know when there would be a gun attack and we were caught up in this situation but not by choice, and it was getting worse. On one particular Monday evening around eight o'clock, a dark, damp, cold night, I remember our youngest child was still in nappies. I stripped off her clothes, washed her and wrapped her in a towel and left her sitting on the floor. The airing cupboard or hot press, as it was then called was upstairs and I went up to get a nappy and pyjamas so I could get her ready for bed. Our other children were doing their homework and Pat was helping them. I had just reached the top of the stairs when this unmerciful bang rang out. I ran downstairs thinking the house was coming in on top of us. The baby was screaming and the children were hysterical. We all lay down on the floor and did not even dare to look at each other. This time it was much stronger gunfire than before. Continual shooting of rifles and machine gun. Words cannot explain what it was like. It is difficult to imagine the scary, eerie sound.

This was the first large-scale attack on the barracks. The Provos (Provisional IRA) had surrounded the village that night and the barracks were attacked from every side. The attack lasted half an hour. Afterwards, there was silence from the guns but screaming from the children, with shouting outside and everybody wondering what had happened. I looked at our baby and she was on her knees. The towel had fallen off her and she was hysterical, tears streaming down her face and body. The other three children were the same, tears streaming down their faces and were sobbing their hearts out, they were in a very distressed state. It was a mixture of shock and emotion and they were too terrified to speak or ask what was happening. It was the most terrifying experience we ever had and I know that everyone who was in Forkhill that night will never forget it. Old people living alone were in shock, children were upset and unable to sleep that night. The next morning at the gable of our house we found sandbags, which were used the night before. There were footprints in the grass just under the window. We knew this because Pat had cut the grass the day before and the cut grass had stuck to their shoes or boots leaving prints, so we knew the position from where the attack was mounted just outside our house. That was the first of many serious attacks, which would hit our village, and after that first experience local people did not want to live with this type of conflict. So when the elections of 1973 came, everyone wanted change and as much as I did not want Pat to become involved in politics, I thought he could help to change what was happening with the backing of a strong SDLP team. It would make life better within our community and in our country so that our children and grandchildren and everyone else's children and grandchildren would have a better future. They would be free to do what they wanted and have peace to do so, so I would stand by him.

Those attacks led to more annoyance and disruption in our community. It brought the security forces out more on patrols and it also encouraged the Provos to use other ways to get their targets. There had been incidents where car bombs were used. Where an abandoned car was one way of luring the security forces into an ambush and maybe sudden death. There were many of these vehicles left parked along the road sides of South Armagh. Loaded with explosives, waiting for the security forces to arrive. It was one of these vehicles, which claimed the lives of two young people from our area. They were with two others who had been driving in the townland of Dromintee when they stopped alongside a van, which had been parked on the side of the road. One of them opened the door of the van and it exploded, resulting in two young people losing their lives and two more being badly injured. One of these lost his eyesight. The incident left the whole community stunned, saddened and heartbroken for the families of the young boys, but it was to become the start of many more tragedies in our area.

Pat's first term in the new Newry and Mourne District Council brought with it very challenging times. The new councillors, with John McAteer as the first chairman, set out to achieve most, if not all of the promises made during the election campaign. Under their control were such things as environmental health, swimming baths, amenities to encourage tourism, the improvement of the areas general appearance, and many other matters such as building control regulations, consulting with the DoE with regard to roads, water and sewage and a direct involvement on a monthly basis regarding planning. So, for the next four years our lives revolved around council meetings. I carried on with bringing up our children as best I could. There was the homework, and this was always a time, when I would wish that Pat was there, just for that help alone. Something would always crop up when he would have time off, and considering that he was still working in Dundalk, he did not have a lot of time to get on with council work. Once home from work he would get his dinner and go off again to meetings. Soon people got to know where he was working and so if they were in Dundalk they would call in to where he worked and discuss whatever problem they had.

However, his employers, although they were delighted that he was elected a councillor, were not too happy about the political involvement. I suppose when you are in business and especially in Dundalk at that time, it was better that you kept your political views to yourself and so Pat soon found himself out of a job. With more time on his hands I thought I could get a few things done around the house that were neglected. But I was so wrong. Very soon he was appointed to various other committees and we saw less of him than before. It took a lot of getting used to for the children and myself. Those meetings would go on until eleven and even twelve o'clock and after the children went to bed it was a long night on my own. I know there is always plenty to do when children go to bed, and so when the chores were done the nights were very long waiting for Pat to come home. In those days there wasn't a lot to do socially and sometimes I would get fed up. We would still get the odd burst of gunfire in Forkhill, always when least expected.

I remember putting the children to bed on this particular night and they went straight to sleep. This was rare most of the time, if not all of the time. I spent my nights up and down the stairs threatening to tell their father on them if they didn't go to sleep. However, on this particular night they did sleep and at around ten thirty there was a burst of gunfire. It went on for ages. I ran upstairs to get the children and bring them downstairs to safety. The reason for this was twofold. I would gather them all into the corner next to the wall of the house next door so that we would be away from the windows, and also because our houses were not brick on the upstairs, only plaster board covered with mesh and thistle plaster on the outside. Bullets could easily penetrate them. On that night when I went to get them up I woke the two older children and they rushed downstairs. I pulled the younger one out of bed onto the floor but he kept trying to get back into bed. He was half asleep. I desperately needed to get him down to safety.

These were the sort of things that we were living with. These outbursts of gun fire. It had become so regular that the headmaster at the school had the children trained in such a way that when he hit the desk a sudden thump, they would all lie down on the floor until he told them to get up. That's how sudden the shooting would start, day or night. The children in the village all played in or around their own homes after these attacks, which were aimed at the lookout posts and the barracks. The security forces would come out on patrol. At first they would go house to house and ask if anyone noticed anything suspicious. At the beginning they were friendly enough but then as the attacks became more frequent they became more aggressive, especially towards teenagers and then the adults. Whenever you were travelling and stopped at checkpoints, it became intolerable. Young people took a lot of abuse from the security forces, being stopped and questioned going to and from their work and the same thing happened at night, sometimes kept for ages along the road. It was now getting much worse and young people were getting fed up with the whole situation.

Chapter 6
TOUGH TIMES

After being out of work for some time Pat took a stall in Jonesboro Market. This market was held on Sundays and was becoming very popular and as he was well used to buying and selling and had a few new ideas, he decided to give it a go. If life was tough before, the stall in Jonesboro Market didn't leave it any easier. Our children resented the fact that they had to help. On Sunday morning we were up early and went to Dundalk for Mass at eight o'clock. Then came home, had our breakfast and then loaded the trailer with the items that were to be sold in the market. Going to the market was okay but to get into the yard, get space, get the stall up, unload the trailer and then get the car and trailer to the car park, then get back and display the goods, was something of an ordeal. I went there as well and believe me, I heard language that I had never heard before. You see, all the traders arrived at the same time and every one of them was doing exactly as we were doing, so you can imagine what it was like with tempers flaring. Then the same procedure at the end of the day before we could get home. The children hated it, but they didn't mind counting the money at the end of the day.

Two years after the election and the Troubles were not getting any better. Pat was still as busy as ever with his council work and we hardly saw him. The children were into new classes. Our eldest one moved on to St Joseph's Secondary School in Crossmaglen. Pat represented Crossmaglen in everything that was possible and the vast majority of his supporters were from the Crossmaglen and surrounding areas. A candidate who ran for Republican Clubs in the Crossmaglen area was elected but he never took his seat when the council formed in nineteen seventy three, so Pat was the only representative. However, there were still people who resented him and the SDLP. Every person is entitled to their own political views. We all wanted peace and wanted the same freedom for our country. The majority of us wanted a peaceful solution but others resorted to violence and it seemed better to keep your political views to yourself as far as those people were concerned.

A good example was when one of our children had made the daunting change from primary to secondary school. Four weeks into the first term at St Joseph's he was obviously not too excited about the new school, which is only natural for any child changing from primary school to secondary. As usual he got the bus every morning, as did all the others from the village that had started school at the same time, and as far as we were concerned everything was fine. A few more weeks went by and one morning there was a knock on the door at around nine thirty. I opened the door and to my surprise there stood a man who was a bus driver and was responsible for the children travelling from our area to school in Crossmaglen. He told me our child was having problems and was going through a difficult time from certain individuals However, he informed me that the reason for it all was because of Pat's political involvement. I thanked him very much and he left.

I was angry and annoyed that one of our children was suffering as a consequence of Pat's political beliefs. The hours passed until the children came home from school. I was on my own. Pat as usual was away on council business. I asked myself how this could happen to one of our children, me who was born and reared in Crossmaglen. The Crossmaglen I grew up in where I spent the happiest days of my life. Teachers who had come to teach us loved the place, as did builders, doctors, bank managers and policemen. All who were ever involved with Crossmaglen in any way had only good memories of it and of its friendly people who would go out of their way to help a stranger and make them feel at home.

The next morning Pat and I went to see the headmaster at St Joseph's with the necessary information we got from our child. The headmaster was surprised when we told him what was going on. As far as he was concerned, if there was any problem at the school, he would know about it, but as it happened, he didn't know and refused to believe there was a problem. We decided to take our child from the school and seek a transfer to St Paul's High School, Bessbrook. This was not an easy task. We went to see the headmaster at St Paul's and explained to him what had happened. He was willing to accept our son providing the headmaster in Crossmaglen had no objection and would sign a release form. The headmaster in Crossmaglen would not sign a release form, because in so doing he would be admitting that there was a problem in his school and that he, the headmaster, was not aware of it. It took a long time to get it sorted out but eventually we did.

The headmaster in Crossmaglen began an investigation and was astounded when he found out what was going on. Finally he signed the release form and our child settled into the new school and had no problems. Our next child went to St Paul's and did encounter some problems at an early stage but the headmaster soon had the problem under control. Again this was because of Pat being involved in politics and the party he represented. Another of our children went to Crossmaglen and under the new headmaster and his teachers did extremely well.

Newry and Mourne District Council was one of the first councils to introduce power sharing. When John McAteer completed his term of office, it was time to select a new chairman, and the man to take over the helm of the council was John McEvoy or "Big John" as he was affectionately known. Business continued at council level and many of the new regulations were being put into practice. They were all doing a good job but we were still having problems in our area. If it wasn't the Provos it was the security forces and our lives seemed to revolve around both. There were rumours of checkpoints mounted by the Provos and so you were worried about being stopped by them and then you were always sure of being stopped by the security forces. You prayed to God that you wouldn't be stopped somewhere between both. If that ever happened then you wouldn't have to worry any more as you would never get away from there alive! Having said that, I always worried just the same as any other mother when our children or any member of the family were out at night. We all got on with our lives and tried as best we could to ignore what was going on.

There were functions where the councillors and their wives were invited, but I wouldn't go because of the way things were around our area. You never knew when there might be an attack on the barracks or worse still another machine gun attack. I would not leave the children or leave anyone to babysit. Anyway, council functions were all new to me and to be honest I didn't really mind. I didn't get involved socially in those early days.

Chapter 7
TALENT SHOW

Pat has a lovely singing voice and I remember when he worked in Dundalk a good friend of ours at the time entered him in a competition organised by RTE. I think it was called "Search for a Star" or something like that and it was held in Castlebellingham Hotel. Granny Toner, Pat's mother loved to hear Pat singing and in his early school days she took him, when he was very young, to Belfast to take part in auditions for Hughie Green's show "Opportunity Knocks". This was a very popular show on television; Granny would have loved to have seen Pat get on the show. Unfortunately it was not to be. The Castlebellingham show started at nine o'clock and we left early so as to be there in good time. We arranged to meet our friends whom we brought along to give Pat support, as the winner would be judged on the applause of the audience. We arrived far too early and as Pat was very nervous Christy suggested that a drink would settle his nerves so he bought him a brandy. Neither of us drank alcohol at the time. After two, Pat's nerves were beginning to settle. There were thirty contestants altogether and Pat was number thirty on the list!

He was to sing two songs and his choice was "Mother Macree" and "Sweet Sixteen", his two favourites, and he could sing them very well. However, on this occasion something went terribly wrong. He had his sheet music that he handed to the pianist and his first song was "Mother Macree" She started the introduction for "Mother Macree" and Pat started to sing "Sweet Sixteen". The pianist stopped him and he started again into "Sweet Sixteen". She stopped him again and this time he told her that she was wrong, and so she did not argue with him, but proceeded to play Sweet Sixteen and so Pat began again only this time it was "Mother Macree" he sang. An argument went on between them for a few minutes with Pat insisting that she played the wrong song and the pianist insisting that she was right. It was hilarious and the place was coming down with laughter that had people doubled up in their seat- everyone that is except me. If I could have found a small mouse hole I would have got into it some way and disappeared.

Pat did not win the best soloist but he did win the best comedy act! After that I said I would never go anywhere with him again, The real reason was, as explained before, that I would not feel very happy leaving any young girl alone with the children in case of an attack.

1973 was an eventful year for explosions and tragedies but still everyone kept hoping and praying that there might be a way to stop the killing and bombing. With the first year over, the new chairman settled in and the meetings proceeded, but business took a long time and usually would go on late. Sometimes up until midnight and in some cases even later. This was because if some councillors left the meeting early others had to stay on to make up a quorum so that meetings could be completed. If some councillors had no further business to discuss they would go to the chairman's room across the hall from the council chamber, which was where the Chairman entertained guests and visitors who came to the area. It was also a place to go and have a drink at the chairman's invitation. Although a lot of the time some councillors would go in and sit there if any item on the agenda did not relate to their particular area. When the meetings were over the chairman would open up the drinks cabinet and there, the various discussions would take place over a relaxing drink.

With John Mc Evoy at the helm those nights became extremely entertaining with great singsongs that lasted into the wee small hours. I was, or I think I was, a very understanding wife. I was not used to this procedure and I worried about Pat being late. That perhaps he would get caught up in one of the road blocks. Mind you, had I known then that a lot of the time was spent in the chairman's room, I might not have worried at all, but when you are on your own it is surprising what goes through your head, and a lot of things did go through my head. I thought of the threats he received during the election campaign and the abuse that he was given. There were fourteen steps on our stairs and on those late nights as I waited for him to come in I would start on the top step of the stairs and I would sit for a while. Then I would move down a few steps and sit there for a while and I would say "please God send him home safe." I would move down a few more steps and get so angry with him for getting involved with the council and for putting the children and me in this position. Then I would hear his car and say thank God for sending him home safe. Those were the times when you just could not think straight.

A few people including Pat and I got involved with starting a social evening for senior citizens as there were a lot of people, some who lived alone, in the area around Forkhill and on the outskirts. The idea was good but there was a problem finding somewhere suitable where we could have a night and make them a cup of tea and then have a sing-song and a bit of a dance and help them to meet other people. The most suitable place was the dinner hall in the school and so during a meeting the committee asked for volunteers to go and speak to the priest and ask his permission to use the school. The curate at that time was Father O'Neill or 'White' Father O'Neill as he was called because of his white hair and to distinguish him from another priest we had some time before. Three of us went to see him in the Parochial House in Mullaghbawn, Mima Campbell, Berna Toner and myself. We explained to him what we wanted to do, but he refused at once and said under no circumstances would he allow the school to be used.

There were a few heated exchanges and while the others remained calm, I became angry and told him that he could keep his school. I said we would start our nights and hold them one week in my house and the next in someone else's and so on. Eventually he said "Alright woman, I will give the school, but don't go at it like a bull". He said he had seen far too many of these things started only to fall by the wayside but he gave the school and the social night was held once a week. It was a great success and many great nights were held there with much fun and laughter.

It progressed so much that there was a need for bigger premises and just a short time after that, the Courthouse in Forkhill was up for sale and so this was an ideal challenge for Pat to see if the council would buy it and perhaps Forkhill would have its own community centre. The plan did work and with Pat's direct involvement and with support from other councillors we got our community centre. A transformation from the courthouse to become the first council provided community centre in the rural area of Northern Ireland. Little did Father O'Neill think that on the night of our visit to him asking for the dinner hall in the school that it would be the beginning of what had become a very successful community centre. It was also a great senior citizens club and as the original community centre became too small for the growing community, a new centre was proposed at council level by Pat. With the support of local councillors and other councillors from outside the area, a new purpose built centre was developed on a green field site given by the local GAA club. This is fully used by the whole community. We are not involved now as younger people are running it, but we are both very proud to have been involved at the start and to see it prosper.

I did not go out much in the early days of Pat's involvement at council, but now that the children were getting bigger, there was less pressure on me and so as the SDLP convention was coming up in January, Pat thought it would be nice if we could attend and that I would meet a lot of people. I was reluctant and didn't want to even consider going, but my Sister Kathleen who had always been with me when the children were younger, said she would come and stay and look after them. I knew she would do that as she knew how I felt about going away, because of what might happen, and although it would start on Friday through to Sunday, I said I would go on Saturday and come back Sunday. Her words to me were that nothing was going to happen in a day, so I decided yes, I would go. The conference was being held in the Europa Hotel in Belfast and it was an occasion to meet all the members from different areas and a chance to meet the leader of the party, John Hume and associate with others who helped to make the party a great success.

With his involvement in local government and being elected to represent South Armagh, Pat loved to go and I did appreciate the fact that to get to where he was in local government and the SDLP at that time he had every right to be there. He deserved it after what he went through and what we as a family, all went through. He could talk with his colleagues and the party leader and feel he was a part of what might come in the future.

The 18th of January 1975 was a beautiful morning and I got up early to get as much done as I could before we left. There was the washing as usual, then tidying up and leaving the children's clothes out for them to get dressed. Deep down I was still reluctant, but I knew Kathleen would take care of them all as she had been with them for so long and they loved her. Although she was now left school and had a job, she still came to us at the weekend and assured me everything would be all right and I could trust her. I said to myself it was only for one night, so to leave lunchtime Saturday and come back Sunday evening, what could go wrong? The children are off school and nothing can happen. Reluctantly, I packed the weekend bag and was ready to leave. I kissed them all goodbyes, the three older children and the baby. I was only going to Belfast but the way I felt leaving them you would think I was never going to see them again. However with Kathleen's assurance that she would take good care of them we went on our way.

Chapter 8
TRAGIC DEATH OF YOUTH

We arrived at the Europa Hotel. The splendour of the place was fantastic. A different world completely and one I was not used to. We made our way to reception to book in and get our room and it seemed too good to be true. I thought the reception area and what I had just experienced was something out of this world. And then the bedroom! I thought about home, our bedroom, a double bed, a cot beside the bed, clothes everywhere, and toys scattered around the floor! The back bedroom, which was the boys' room, had all the clutter and toys that are part of a boy's room, Action Man, cars and football stickers. I thought of the little front room of our daughter's, it had every thing a little girl would have. Tiny Tears doll, pram, tea set, hair bands, dressing up clothes and all the things girls have in their bed room. Here I was, no clutter, no children, just a beautiful room with everything perfect, however I still felt sad.

The conference started early and as I settled in, Pat went down to see what was going on and if there was anything interesting. I joined him later on and we listened to some of the various motions that were being discussed . The dinner dance was to start at eight o'clock so I went to have a shower and to get ready. Just before I went down I phoned home to see if everything was alright and Kathleen assured me that the children were fine and said not to worry. Everything was quiet and for us to enjoy ourselves. The dance was brilliant and we had a great night. We met our friends and made new ones and talked to everyone we knew and sang into the early hours of the morning. I want to quote from my diary, which I started when Pat was elected. "Sat 18 Jan 1975. Pat and I attended the SDLP Conference in the Europa Hotel. A most interesting and educational day. The dinner dance and later cabaret was very good and we had a most enjoyable day and evening, but something was to mar all this".

Sunday morning we got up and went down and had breakfast and then we went to Mass along with all the others who like ourselves wanted to go. It was in the heart of Belfast where there was so much terror and unrest but that day it seemed peaceful and quiet. The Priest read out that there was a peace rally to be held at the City Hall and some of us decided on the way back that we would go. Pat stayed at the conference, so along with Marie McEvoy, Paddy O'Hanlon and his girlfriend Anne, (who was later to become his wife) a few others and I went to the peace rally. I had never seen so many people come together for one purpose and one purpose only. Peace. Everyone wanted peace, and the message was clear. It was so touching and when the rally was over and we were walking away, Paddy gave us all a tulip. He had bought the tulips from a lady who was selling them as we were leaving the peace rally. I felt then that there had to be peace because so many people wanted it so much, but we were so very wrong. It was only just the beginning of the hatred, the bitterness and the violence. We walked back to the Europa and as we approached the entrance we noticed that there were a lot of reporters and television crews.

Paddy went through the door first, then Anne, I was next and as I did so, reporters were crowding around Paddy and I heard them ask him if Pat Toner was with him. He replied "No, is there something wrong?" They said yes, that a Toner child had been killed in Forkhill. I was right behind Paddy at this time and I passed out. As I came round all I could hear were people saying, "Will somebody find Pat Toner?" I was crying now and nobody could tell me anything. All I knew was that a child had been killed in Forkhill and his name was Pat Toner and I thought dear, dear God. I knew I should never have left them. I did not want to come. Then Pat came. He had been at one of the meetings and told me it was bad, but it was not our child. It was John and Pen Toner's little Pat. Kathleen had been on the phone trying to contact us to let us know what had happened and to tell us it was not our child. Oh dear God it was just as bad because what I felt then I knew another person was feeling such pain, only far worse. This tragedy was real for them.

We got our things together and went home. From my diary "Sun 19th Jan. As the conference on this day did not really have anything to interest me I decided to go to the City Hall and take part in the peace rally being held today. Such a large crowd of people turned out and surely we could see that peace was wanted, but at the time of the peace rally, in our hometown Forkhill, little Pat Toner was killed in a booby trap explosion." We immediately left for Forkhill.

When we arrived in Forkhill, the security forces had blocked off the village and they would not allow us to get to our house. We sat for a while pleading for them to let us get home to our children and while we were there my other sister arrived from Bessbrook. She had heard the news and came straight to Forkhill assuming that it was our child. She had tried to get to our house and had left to try another way but then came back. Eventually with us all in tears, they let us home. My God, when I saw our house, the front window was out, the glass in the front door was gone and there was twisted wood around the door. We went in and I shall never ever forget the sight of our children. They were in shock and poor Kathleen broke down and cried her heart out.

I will again quote from my diary "My heart went out to Mrs Toner and John. Words cannot explain how they must feel. For a few moments back in Belfast I felt pain when I first heard the news and thought that it was one of our children. This is a horrible and senseless killing. I hope some day, someone will pay the price."

The whole village was stunned. How could anyone in his or her right mind do such a thing? Again my diary speaks. "Mon 20th Jan. A terrible thing has happened. Any child or children could have been killed and our hearts went out to John and Pen Toner on their great loss. I still wonder many days if those responsible will ever live with peace of mind. The funeral came home to Forkhill from Daisy Hill Hospital". Tues. 21st Jan: "Wee Pat Toner was buried in Mullaghbawn. Never has there been such a tragic, sad, sickening sight as what has happened. This diary at this stage does not hold happy memories for me. Maybe when the years in it are filled, someone along the way will pay for what they did".

Our village tried to get back to normal. Our thoughts from then on were what is normal going to be? We had our first taste of gunfire, our first taste of serious machine gun attack, our first taste of one of our young people killed by a landmine explosion. What can we expect next? From now on our children really lost their freedom. They were not allowed to go anywhere away from home. Kept out of fields. Not allowed to wander too far away from the house. No more going down the Urnai Loanin. No more going to the Waterfall. No more into Haughey's field. No more going to the Planting (area of woodland and trees) and no more going around the Bog Road. All out of bounds. These places were so popular with all the children of the village and they enjoyed going to them.

However life went on. On Wednesday January 22nd at a meeting of Newry and Mourne District Council on the proposal of councillor Pat Toner, it was agreed that a peace demonstration be arranged for Sunday January 26th in Soho Car Park in Newry to give people a chance to show that they sympathised with the Toner family, and that they did not want violence but peace. The village of Forkhill and its people had to try and come to terms with all that had happened in our community and everyone did try very hard to accept that we now had no control of what was going on around us. More patrols and more stopping cars and more searches and most of all the not knowing what might happen next or when there would be another attack on the barracks. Or even more landmines.

The last thing I wanted was to go out anywhere but we had forgotten about an invitation which we received to attend a variety concert in St Joseph's High School in Crossmaglen, Pat was on the Board of Governors at St Joseph's and after we received the invitation I noticed that Maggie Barry was appearing in concert on Saturday 25th January. I remember saying to Pat when the invitation came how much I wanted to go. Maggie Barry was a part of my childhood days and she had left Ireland to go to America after a talent scout discovered her. This was her first time back in Crossmaglen, a place where she was so familiar and where she had lived just a few miles outside the town. With all that had happened in the past weeks I had forgotten all about it until another councillor and his wife rang to say we could travel with them. It was a very difficult decision to make as to whether we would go or not, but I so wanted to see Maggie and to speak with her. Saturday night came and I got Karen Toner to babysit for us. Karen lived just across the road from us. She was no relation but a daughter of our good friends Tom and Berna and she was also a cousin of wee Pats. I knew if anything went wrong she had only to ring her mother and she would look after things.

It was a very cold night and before I left, Karen offered me her new coat as it was lovely and warm and she said it looked nice on me and so I wore it. We all went to Crossmaglen and no doubt Maggie Barry did herself proud and she was the same Maggie that I remembered singing on The Square in Crossmaglen on a fair day. When the show was over we were then invited to go to Fintan Callan's pub. Fintan had recently bought the pub in Crossmaglen and it was known for traditional music evenings. There were a lot of local people who came that night to talk with Maggie and to recollect old times and she was her old self as she sang and drank her Guinness. It was as if she had never been away. Everyone that had known her from the old days made their way to Fintan's pub that night and no one was turned away. The locals slagged the hell out of her and fair play to Maggie, as always, she gave back as good as she took. Not only did Maggie turn up but there was also a full supporting cast of famous singers and musicians. Crossmaglen, as usual, welcomed her home and they did her proud. It was raining heavy outside but no one really cared about what the weather was like as the craic was too good.

It had turned three thirty as we left the pub and as we went outside we realised that after the rain there was a severe frost. We could not keep our feet on the ground and as we were driving up Moley's Hill heading for Fords Cross and Forkhill, the car left the road at the bad bend and headed straight for the hedge. It skidded and ended up with the back wheels dangling over the hedge, above a drop of six feet into a field. Pat and the other councillor were in the front of the car and his wife and I were in the back. After the initial shock we burst into laughter. The next thing the car started to sway backwards and the laughing stopped. There we sat, not a word spoken because at this stage any sudden movement and the car and its occupants would have ended up in the field below. We sat there for what seemed an eternity and eventually a young man came along and offered his help. One by one we got out of the car. The men first and then very gingerly the other lady and I. The young man said he lived just up the road and went home to get his father's tractor and a rope to pull the car out of the hedge. We waited, but he never came back. It was an awful night. I cannot remember a night as cold, nor can I remember one since. We could not keep our feet on the ground as it was so slippery.

I have often heard the saying "Ducks couldn't walk." Well, in our case we couldn't walk as the frost was so bad. Finally a car came along, stopped and the driver got out and came over to us. Seeing what had happened he went back to his car and got us a rope, which we hooked to a nearby tree and used it as a means to hold on to as we crossed the road. That man was none other than the famous David Hammond and his passenger that night was Joe Burke. They had been performing with Maggie Barry in the hall and went to Fintan's for something to eat and stayed for the craic.

Eventually at around six o'clock in the morning a young man on his way to Crossmaglen delivering the Sunday papers to Peggy Martins, stopped and said he would get help when he got to Cross which he did, and the car was pulled from the hedge and we finally got home. Because we were out in the damp and cold, the coat that I had borrowed from Karen had shrunk and what started off as a long coat was now a three quarter length coat. She was very good about it and was glad to know that we were safe and sound. We met David Hammond, the famous musician, during the Tommy Makem festival of folk music in Mullaghbawn some years later and he told us he remembered that night very well and we had a great laugh about it all.

On Sunday January 26th there was a large attendance in Soho Car Park in Newry. This was the peace demonstration. One of the first in Northern Ireland, where people came to express their horror and disgust at what had happened to the little boy in Forkhill. It was also to show their support for peace in our community and for peace in our country. All members of the council were there, as well as Clergy from all denominations and we all joined in the prayers for peace. Together we prayed for John and Pen Toner and the Toner family that God would give them comfort and in some way help them to come to terms with their great loss.

Life got back to normality but the thoughts of the recent tragedy were still in our minds. Life was difficult in that there was always the fear of landmines and we now had more army foot patrols. The soldiers were very busy on the ground and there were more and more checkpoints. The children from the village who went to school up the back road past the barracks were now in constant danger. At any time there could be an attack, and much worse, children walking into the village to attend school were in danger also because you just did not know where landmines were planted. They could lie there for ages and locals would not even know that they were there. No consideration was ever given to the fact that children might be on their way home from school when any of these attacks happened, or for that matter any person going to the shop, young or old.

In a statement issued after the first official meeting of Newry and Mourne District Council, Pat stated that he was delighted that Enterprise Ulster had decided to go ahead with their £30,000 scheme for a play area in the Ardross Housing Estate in Crossmaglen. He hoped that this would be the start of better things to come in the future as regards playing facilities in estates throughout the South Armagh area, which in his opinion had been sadly neglected in the past. The majority of people moving into housing estates were young married couples with children and safe playing areas for them were a necessity for all estates, even the smallest. How right he was. Crossmaglen had its share of attacks as well and there was a great need for safe play areas so that children could have fun and that parents knew where they were. This play area was the first of many that he had proposed and with the help and support of his colleagues at council level. Another resolution which he had, was calling for the support of the other 25 district councils to change the planning laws. This asked the other councils to call on the appropriate government department to effect an immediate easing of the restrictive regulations with regard to rural housing planning policy. It stated: "It is our opinion that if this is not immediately done a severe depopulation of certain rural areas is inevitable".

For Pat, rural planning was one of the most important issues ever to be discussed. From the first day he set foot in the council chamber he fought and fought very hard with the Planners with regard to planning permission in rural areas. It annoyed him so much when young people who wanted to build a house near their parents, or on land which their parents had given them, were turned down. There were farmers who had worked their farms all their lives to build them up so that a son or daughter would eventually get married and take over the running of the farm. Or in some cases where a mother or father was ill and therefore needed help with the day to day running of the farm. Site meetings were called and in discussions with the Planners, the problems were resolved.

There is not a road in South Armagh that Pat was not involved with regarding planning permission. So many young couples came to our house to talk to Pat about their planning application. They would be so full of enthusiasm about their new house only to have their hopes dashed when their planning permission was refused. I remember how very annoyed Pat would be when this happened and in particular with the chief planning officer. Pat always had difficulty coming to terms with the decisions made by the Planners, believing it was a case of being dictated to, as to where a person could or could not have a home, by those who did not understand life in rural areas. There was a time also when we had our fellow countrymen doing the same.

There was a certain part of the Culloville - Crossmaglen area where the Provos had control of planning permission that ran the west side of the Concession Road from Ballinacarry to Culloville. It was classified as an operational area and therefore no planning permission was allowed. They decided that no houses would be built there. There was a person who had been told that he could not build and came to our house with a letter that was supposed to come from the PIRA, second battalion, Crossmaglen. It may not have been so, but he never built his house. There were other areas in South Armagh where, because of pressure from Provos, people were not allowed to develop either private or business properties.

Pat always maintained that this was not liberation but dictatorship and he got the chance to go on television, the Today-Tonight programme which was discussing the problems with regard to planning, stated that "it was wrong for PIRA to fight for peoples rights and freedom from British rule and at the same time dictate where people could or could not build." He raised the issue at council level and was accused by a Sinn Fein councillor of not knowing what he was talking about and that what he was saying was totally untrue, even though Pat had a copy of the letter which was sent to one of the developers, warning him to cease his development. Some of these developments are still there; some reached roof level and are to this very day still unfinished.

The heading in a report by journalist Ted Oliver, in the Belfast Telegraph on Tuesday, December 11th 1973 read, "Informers will be remembered here for twenty years". The article also described an interview with a Crossmaglen resident who agreed that informers would indeed be remembered for a very long time "it's that kind of place, Crossmaglen". The article also described how in the Fifties, Crossmaglen Fair was the "the best in Ulster". In the Sixties the people were starting again to make the world–famous Carrickmacross lace, and a prominent Crossmaglen resident even went so far as to describe the town as "the Killarney of the North". In October 1973, however, things were very different, with the Provisional IRA warning, "keep a considerable distance from all troops in the village because of the danger of civilian casualties in future attacks."

True enough, this applied to most towns and villages throughout South Armagh and yes, informers would be remembered for a long time. Informer (definition-one who informs, one who makes a practice of informing against others for the sake of gain) what about proof? How do you prove someone is an informer? What actions constitute being labelled an informer? In many cases there was no evidence at all. To be labelled an informer made you a target for the Provos. It had become a very dangerous word to use in South Armagh. It also left any person who had a reason to go to the barracks in a very vulnerable position. Questions could be asked, "Why should anyone need to go to the barracks?" After all, that was the RUC station. It was also the base for the security forces and the perception was no one had any need to go there. If you did, you were or could be accused of informing.

There were many reasons why people had to go to the barracks. The most usual one being that if a person was stopped by a patrol and did not have their driving licence or perhaps some form of identification at hand, they would have their name taken and asked to bring either their licence or motor insurance or both and produce them at their nearest RUC barracks within so many days from the time they were stopped. This created a big problem for a lot of people and more so for people living in Crossmaglen. There was no way you would consider going to the barracks in Crossmaglen. Anyone from that area that happened to get stopped and who had to produce any form of identification, always asked if they could do so at Forkhill Barracks; because Pat was an elected public representative, many members of the public called at our house and asked him to accompany them to the barracks. In doing this no one could accuse him or her of informing. This was how serious it was and how frightened people were at the time.

My grandfather Tommy Clarke

My grandmother Annie Clarke

Grandmother in doorway of shop

Fair Day Crossmaglen 1950's

Fair Day Crossmaglen 1950's

THE SQUARE, CROSSMAGLEN.

The Square, Crossmaglen 1950's

Christine with a friend on right. Outside grandmother's shop

Pat and Christine's wedding day, Preston, England

Christine and Pat during a talent competition

Armagh Minor Team - Ulster Champions 1957

Abbey Grammar, Corn na N-Og - Winners 1954

Sniper window lookout

Bank and Court House, Crossmaglen.

Belfast Bank and Court House, The Square, Crossmaglen

● CAMPAIGN ... One of the anti-RUC posters which has appeared in Forkhill

Phone warnings over RUC Christmas parties

By **Phelim McAleer**

COUNCILLORS and community leaders in south Armagh have had threatening phone calls allegedly from the IRA warning them not to attend RUC Christmas functions, the *Irish News* can reveal.

Forkhill SDLP councillor Pat Toner has told how he was warned that, if he went to a local RUC Christmas party, the IRA would organise a "special function" for him later.

The threats, which police say have·been made to a number of councillors, community leaders and teachers in south Armagh, are part of a new campaign against the RUC in the area.

Mr Toner is calling on the IRA to state if the threats came from a genuine republican source or were the work of a crank.

Signs condemning the RUC as "92 per cent protestant, 100 per cent loyalist" have recently appeared on telegraph poles outside south Armagh villages.

Every year police stations across Northern Ireland invite local representatives, journalists, prominent citizens and community groups to Christmas dinners or parties.

It is believed this is the first year threats have been directed towards those who attend.

Mr Toner says it was strange that, in Belfast, republicans were fighting to be included in talks and invited to conferences, but in south Armagh were trying to stop any contact with the RUC.

"It is recognised that the RUC will have to be changed but these changes are not going to happen overnight. Will it change the situation by threatening ordinary people going to visit police stations as part of their official function?" he asked.

He said it was strange that the first year there is a ceasefire, was the first year people are being threatened about attending such functions.

"I got a phone call last Sunday week at 6.25pm and the voice asked me was I going to this police function. I said I was and the man said if I did they would organise one for me later."

"I answered him back and asked where it would be held but he said i would find out."

Mr Toner says he attended the police dinner despite the threats.

"I learned if you gave into threats as a councillor, people just walk over you," he said.

Newspaper clipping from a local newspaper

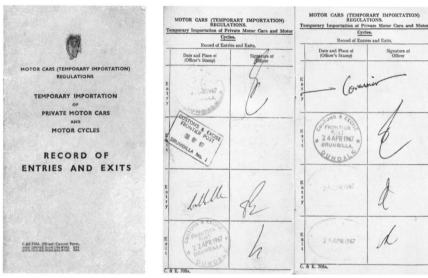

Auto mobile records of entries and exits book, to and from The Republic Of Ireland

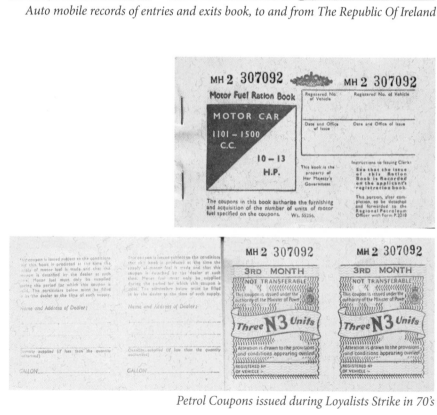

Petrol Coupons issued during Loyalists Strike in 70's

Ready for Festival, Forkhill

Pony and trap competition, during South Armagh Festival in Forkhill

South Armagh

Forkhill Barracks mortared

POWs nn Fein

'EMENT has been smug-
Republican News by the
ise Prison.

n Portlaoise Prison, wish to
regarding this year's Sinn
d the policy of abstention-
elections.

rty and those imprisoned
it of Irish freedom, within
is constitutional issue in a
d forthright manner, with
ld beliefs being respected

/ prisoners, we accept the
cil to speak on our behalf
lecisions of the IRA Con-

-Fheis and the major issue
publicised in all the news-
mann in the 32 Counties
motions to go before the
wed adequate time, in ad-
the total membership to
a clear two-thirds majority
nd the policy of abstent-
. The republican POWs in
lecision.

trength of feeling and sin-
e change of policy. We sal-

A BRITISH ARMY HELICOPTER carrying enemy soldiers narrowly escaped destruction when IRA Volunteers
launched six 50lb mortar bombs at the Forkhill RUC/
British army barracks in South Armagh on Tuesday
evening, November 18th.

The mortar tubes had earlier been fitted to a van and,
shortly before 5pm, were
driven into McCreesh Park in
Forkhill. The Volunteers lin-
ed the mortars up and prepared the firing set. As the
Wessex helicopter took off,
the mortars fired, hitting the
base and damaging the perimeter fence and buildings
inside the compound.

CHECKPOINT FIRED ON

A few hours later, an IRA act-

ive service unit opened fire on the
permanent British army checkpoint at Clady on the Tyrone-
Donegal border.

According to the West Tyrone
Brigade of the IRA, which claimed responsibility for the operation, four IRA Volunteers fired
"upwards of 60 high-velocity shots
at crown forces as they entered
the checkpoint".

COLLABORATOR TARGETED

The garage and car showrooms
of a Portglenone businessman, Joe

Reed, were the target last week of
an IRA bomb attack.

On Thursday evening, November 13th, Volunteers from the
IRA's North Antrim Brigade placed a 100lb bomb in the premises
at Townhill Road, Portglenone.
The bomb failed to explode and
was eventually dismantled by British engineers.

Following the attack, the IRA's
North Antrim Brigade said that
Reed "regularly services crown
forces vehicles, particularly those
belonging to the RUC's Divisional
Mobile Support Unit".

Also on Thursday, a paint-
ing contractor from Castlewellan,
County Down, publicly announ-
ced that he will no longer be
carrying out any further work for
the crown forces.

SOLDIER INJURED

One British soldier was injured
when IRA Volunteers in Derry
detonated a remote-control bomb
on Thursday night, November
13th.

The anti-personnel mine had
been hidden in a hedge close to
gates leading into St Patrick's
Church a short time before the
attack. The IRA engineer withdrew 50 yards and waited for an
expected British army foot-patrol
to pass.

Shortly after 7pm, a 12-man
foot-patrol moved up the Bun-
crana Road. At 7.10pm, the
device was detonated, blasting one
soldier several yards and injuring
him.

ALLOWED TO RETURN

The IRA's East Tyrone Brigade
has issued a statement saying that
Francie Coleman, from Ardboe,
one of several men ordered from
the area some time ago by the
IRA, has been allowed to return.

The IRA said:

"Following representations
from a number of people in Ardboe who guaranteed that Coleman
will receive expert medical treatment, we have reviewed our position. Coleman can return but we
will carefully monitor his behaviour. This is his final chance."

DUTCH LIBERALISM GIVES WAY TO POLITICAL EXPEDIENCY IN McFARLANE-KELLY EXTRADITION CASE

British pressure on Dutch

FOLLOWING the decision taken by the Dutch Justice Ministry to extradite Gerry Kelly and Brendan McFarlane, their

reme Court decision. Clearly
under intense British pressure not

Article from the Republican News, Nov 1986

Provos patrol countryside

Pony and trap competition, Forkhill

Main Street, Forkhill

*Chairman, Newry and Mourne Council, dressed as chieftain,
for World Pipe Band Competition during Kingdom of Mourne Festival 1985*

Provos patrol country roads

Provos missile launcher

Local residents open a border road

Left to right, Mr. Willie John McBride, Mrs. J. Crilly (deceased), Councillor Pat Toner, and Mr. Victor Haslett

Warrenpoint Gala Week - Left to right, Warrenpoint Gala Queen, Councillor John Tinnelly (deceased), Chairman Pat Toner, Christine Toner and her son David

Willie Carson, right, Senior partner in Price Waterhouse, hands over the deeds of Newry Canal to Councillor Pat Toner Chairman of Newry and Mourne District Council. Purchase of Newry Canal for two guineas

Newry and Mourne District Council 1973 - Elected Councillors to the new Newry and Mourne District Council with Chairman John McAteer

Elected Councillors, returned, Newry Mourne District Council 1977 with Chairman John McEvoy and officials

Former MP for South Armagh, Eddie Richardson, making a presentation at Forkhill - From Left Delia Murphy and Pat Toner, with Peter Murphy in centre and Jim Flynn on the right

World Pipe Band Competition Kilkeel 1985

1985-86 Councillor Pat Toner, Chairman,
Newry and Mourne District Council

Councillor Pat Toner, Chairman of Newry and Mourne District Council,
presents a Newry and Mourne Plaque to Mr. Peter Tierney, Chairman of Ring
of Gullion Branch of Comhaltas Aoltoiri Eireann. Also in group Mr. Jim Flynn,
left, and Mr. Raymond Turley, Chief Tourist and Recreation Officer.

Pat Toner, John Hume, Tipp O'Neill - Washington DC. Oct 1985

Watch Tower, South Armagh

To Pat Toner
Enjoyed seeing you in Washington
my best Ted Kennedy, DC Sr

Pat Toner meets Ted Kennedy, Oct 1985

Snooker match Davis and Taylor 13 Feb 1986, Sports Centre Newry

Councillor Pat Toner at launch of South Armagh Festival in the 70's

Helicopter from window of Toner's home, Forkhill

Helicopter flies over houses in Fairview Park, Forkhill

Helicopter flies over houses, Forkhill

Helicopter flying close over houses, Forkhill, South Armagh

British Army South Armagh - *Photography by Tonie Carragher*

Watch Tower, South Armagh - *Photography by Tonie Carragher*

Forkhill Barracks , fortified after the arrival of the British Army in late 60's

New Military Fort in Forkhill - Photography by Tonie Carragher

Dismantling of Military Fort , Forkhill

Dismantling of Military Fort Watch Tower, Forkhill, South Armagh

Dismantling of Military Fort Watch Tower, Forkhill, South Armagh

*Three of our grandchildren at Miltary Watch Tower site
overlooking Forkhill (post removal). Military Fort in background*

Forkhill Military Fort cleared internal view (post removal)

NOISE MEASUREMENTS

Equivalent Continuous Sound Level ($L_A$eq) is defined as the level of a notional steady sound which at a given position and over a defined period of time would have the same A weighted acoustic energy as the fluctuating noise. This scale was chosed as it is a convenient method of expressing a fluctuating noise level.

Single Event Noise Level (SEL) is the level which if maintained constant for a period of 1 second would cause the same A weighted sound energy to be received as is actually received from a given noise event. SEL values for contributing noise sources can be considered as individual building blocks being used in the construction of a calculated value of Leq for the total noise.

The SEL for flyovers, take offs and landings at several dwellings outside and close to the grant scheme noise contours in Bessbrook, Crossmaglen and Forkhill were measured. Helicopter movements during the measurement periods and the maximum levels for each movement were also recorded - Appendix 1. The SEL values together with the estimated number of movements in a 12 hour period were used to calculate $L_A$eq (12 hour) for each measurement location - Appendix 2. This method obviates the need for monitoring over complete 12 hour periods.

The number of movements over 12 hour periods were requested from the Ministry of Defense. They replied giving the average monthly movement totals (take offs and landings at each site:)

Bessbrook	3550
Crossmaglen	1350
Forkhill	1280

In June the number of helicopter movements counted at Bessbrook during a 10 hour period starting at 0800 hours was 106. Dividing 3550 by 30 gives an average of 118 movements in 24 hours. It is assumed that 118 movements is typical in a 12 hour period at Bessbrook. Similarly 45 movements in 12 hours at Crossmaglen and 43 at Forkhill.

The following noise monitoring equipment owned by Southern Group Public Health Committee was used:-

> CEL type 393 Precision Computing Sound Level Meter
> B & K type 2218 Precision Sound Level Meter
> B & K type 4230 Calibrator

Extract from the 'Noise from Military Helicopter Report, Newry and Mourne D.C'.

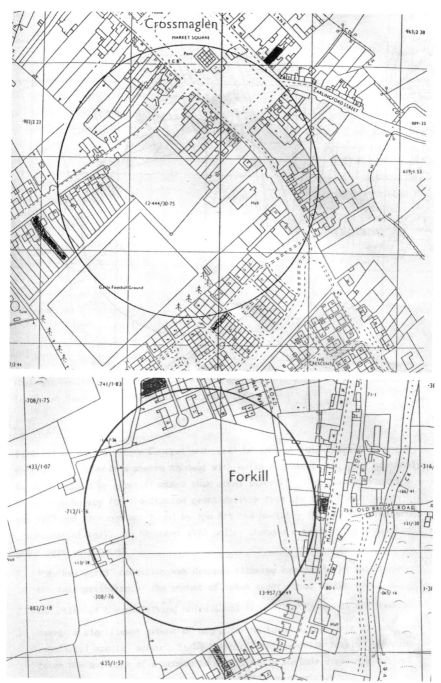

Noise disturbance area from helicopters in Crossmaglen and Forkhill

Panoramic view of Forkhill, South Armagh

Main Street, Forkhill, South Armagh

*His Eminence Cardinal Tomas O Fiaich and
Councillor Pat Toner with The Book of Kells*

THE ABBEY PROJECT
His Eminence Cardinal Tomas O Fiaich
with (left to right) Mr. P. Magennis, Councillor Pat Toner and Rev. Colmcille O.C.S.O,
Rear, Mr. Paddy O'Hanlon, Mr. P. Doherty and Mr. G. Fay

Quinns the Milestone side at Abbey grounds in the 50's including Councillor
Pat Toner, John McKight, Kevin O'Neill, Tony Hadden, Tom McKay and Tom Burke

Chapter 9
LAND OF
HELICOPTER NOISE

Time was rolling on and the situation was not any better. Police cars and army vehicles were now off the roads because they had become targets when travelling from one base to another. Police cars had been attacked and army vehicles were blown up, and so the helicopters were the only means of transportation for the security forces. We lived in the flight line as did other residents, and the constant noise and annoyance of the helicopters flying over our houses became a very big problem. Every child was terrified each time a helicopter came over our houses and the frightened children would run inside screaming. Just think about this. When I was a child, an aeroplane was not very often seen in the skies around South Armagh and when one would appear I remember been brought outside and my granny pointing towards the sky to let me see it. Now we had helicopters many times during the day and night. Can you imagine what this was like for a young child who had not yet even encountered large lorries, buses or trains? The frequent use and the noise and the nuisance of the helicopters were soon to become a battle in itself. We constantly complained time and time again, but to no avail.

The first term of council was almost over and another local government election (1977) was on the way. Some great work had been done in the area, but there was still a lot more to do. Another great achievement for Newry and Mourne District Council was the start of Cross –Border Talks in Newry, described in a local newspaper as "Start of Something Big". Building a bridge across the border in a very real sense was the mission which brought a high- powered delegation from Louth and Monaghan County Councils to Newry, in September, for joint talks with members of Newry and Mourne District Council in the first series of Cross- Border Conferences, which could lead to close co

– operation in the commercial, industrial and tourist spheres.

"No harm can come from having friendly contact with our counterparts in the South" council chairman Arthur Lockhart (1976) said, adding that such co-operation was desirable and made good sense. There was a great potential for the industrial and tourist development of this region, once the present troubles had subsided. That was twenty five years ago when those councillors from Newry and Mourne and Co. Louth and Co. Monaghan, first met and who would have thought then that so many years on, although the path was tough, they succeeded in bringing about all they had proposed to do and much more. Pat was involved in those meetings and as far as I would imagine they would soon celebrate 25 years from their first meeting.

In our village, life was becoming more difficult. There were more and more security checkpoints, and more harassment from the soldiers. They had been fired on so many times that they were now taking a lot of frustration out on the local youth and indeed adults as well. Many young people were being stopped on their way to work and held for ages for no particular reason. This resulted in the person being late for their work. There were soldiers that would become very aggressive but thankfully they did not all behave in the same way. There were always a few really bad boys and they took great pleasure in humiliating people when they were stopped at checkpoints. On one occasion a very good friend of ours was on his way to Newry when the soldiers stopped him. He did not have any identification on him. An unusual thing, given, that he was well used to being stopped and asked for ID. All of us in South Armagh, learned very quickly that it was always better to have some form of ID when travelling as it saved a lot of hassle and a lot of delay at checkpoints. However, this man did not have anything on him at all which would identify him. So the usual procedure occurred –get out of the car, stand along the road - in this case it was on the bridge leading out of the village. Everything was taken out of his car and I mean everything. Seats, mats, anything that was moveable came out and was left along the road. After about an hour, he was still standing on the bridge and had now attracted quite an audience and the regulars of The Welcome Inn could see everything that was going on from the windows of the pub. Angers flared and after asking the soldiers to please put back the car seats and the rest of his belongings- which they refused to do- he lost his head completely and in his frustration began to remove his clothing. Starting with his socks, shirt, trousers and almost his underwear and only then did they decide to let him go. We thought that evening that this disgraceful behaviour from the soldiers was uncalled for, but indeed they were to repeat these actions again and again in the years to come.

The four-year term was up and so the elections of 1977 were fast approaching. A lot of groundwork had been done but there was still a lot more to do. Our home was now an open house and we as a family were starting to come to terms with the fact that Pat was a public representative and that he was committed to the public and the people who voted for him to represent them. So we accepted that we would at times find it difficult with him not always being there when he was needed but we would do our best as a family and give him as much support as we possibly could. There was a lot of canvassing to do and we all helped. We still came up against the troublemakers and those people who did not want peace and as usual they were there shouting and hurling the usual abuse. They would go to any extreme to try to prevent us from canvassing but we hung in there and got on with it. We brought the older children with us once or twice when we were canvassing. It was good for them to see how much people wanted to have peace. After all, they heard us so many times talking about so many different problems that people had. Some had been threatened and were told what they could and could not do. Now they could hear the views of others and could see for themselves why people needed someone to represent them One night they were very annoyed when Pat came home later than usual. He had a party supporter with him and they were delayed because someone had slashed the tyres of his car at Silverbridge and it had taken hours for him to get home. There were quite a lot of incidents like this one which he encountered, but then those involved had no part or no interest in elections at that time and so all they wanted to do was to prevent any change that might deter them from their threatening life style. Pat just got on with it.

Election day arrived. As usual I voted in Forkhill and went to Crossmaglen Polling Station. There was a great turnout this time, not like 1973. People really wanted to show how much they wanted peace. Crossmaglen, like Forkhill had put up with a lot of trouble from the Provos and the security forces and everyone was getting fed up to the teeth with threats from both. The best way they could show their annoyance was to go to the ballot box and vote for what they wanted and that is what they did. My diary read: "Thursday turnout fantastic at Cross, very impressive vote for Pat and the SDLP. Pat won, top of the poll with 900 votes. A fantastic victory for SDLP. Pat not only topped the poll but also took two more SDLP members in, due to proportional representation, where the person could vote 1,2,3 in order of preference for the candidates and the party they supported.

May 1977:- another four years in council started, only this time I would see less of Pat and our children would see less of their father. We carried on as best we could. There was more homework from school and the children, especially the older ones, were working hard. Pat was nominated to various committees of the council and instead of being away from home one or two nights a week it was to become more and more nights of meetings and travelling.

Locally, he was chairman of the South Armagh Festival Committee, which organised a festival every year. This was held around the last week in June leading into the first week of July. The South Armagh Festival gave us all a chance to get out and enjoy ourselves. It was a wonderful time for all of us, young and old. We could forget about the troubles which we had encountered over the past years and for those few weeks, with so many activities organised, it gave each one an opportunity to take part in whatever you were interested in. I know, as a young mother then, it was great to have somewhere to bring your children and the fun that was had was terrific. Art and Maura O' Neill were the proprietors of the Welcome Inn and the yard at the back of the pub was the venue for a lot of the activities. God knows the great night's that were had there and it was so good because with young children and babies it was easy to wheel the pram or pushchair into the yard and see all that was going on instead of sitting at home wondering what was happening and missing all the fun. There were occasions of traditional music, song and story telling every Tuesday night in the Welcome Inn throughout the summer. The Irish night as most people called it. The stories of the now famous John Campbell were popular and we would sit in for a while and listen to it all and then move out to the yard when the crowd started to come in, and play skittles and sing along with all the others to the music coming from inside. Those summer festivals kept us all sane and it is a great pity that they too have diminished.

Chapter 10
TRAGEDIES

We now had many tragedies hanging over us in South Armagh. The murder of the Reavey brothers and the Kings Mills murders and other killings, which had all happened around the same time. Life was becoming more and more depressing. We had to keep some sort of normality about our village but this was almost impossible. The shooting still went on. The targets, the soldiers and the barracks and if you happened to be caught up in this it was a very frightening experience. On one particular evening I had sent our then youngest son to O'Hagan's Shop, which was up the back road, a road that leads up past the barracks. It was a short cut to where you could reach the area of the local school and other housing estates and the shop. From where we lived in Fairview it was easy to go that way instead of having to go down the main street and turn off to reach the back road. It was faster to get to the shop but you had to pass the barracks and with the various attacks, which we endured, we were always afraid of being caught up in one of them.

Our son was on his way home when a gun attack started on the barracks. He was eight years old and had gone on his new bike, which he had just got for Christmas. The shooting started just as he was passing. The soldier in the lookout post shouted at him to lie down on the ground, which he did. The gun fire lasted almost fifteen minutes and all the time that soldier talked down to the child telling him that it would soon be all over. When it was all over, he told him it was safe to get up and go. During the time of the shooting I knew that the child would be on his way back down and I was almost out of my mind. When he did come home he was very frightened but said the soldier talked to him all the time and kept telling him that as long as he kept down he would be alright. The soldiers did not return fire that particular evening. While that incident turned out all right there were others which did not. Bullets had gone through windows of people's houses while their children were playing in the room and but for the protection and grace of God no one was injured.

This term of council brought a lot of new developments throughout the Newry and Mourne area and every one was pulling together at council level to make it all work. But still the element of destruction continued. We were all caught up in this war and the bully boys were making sure that we were part of it, whether we wanted it or not. There were incidents where the soldiers would take young people to the barracks after having stopped them at checkpoints. This was a very frightening experience for any person let alone someone young who had never had any contact with police or indeed was ever inside a barracks. This type of thing had been going on for some time and only came to our attention when parents would call and tell us afterwards what had happened. The very fact that they were seen coming out from the barracks could be very dangerous indeed for the person involved. If the wrong person saw him coming out.

These types of incidents were to be the beginning of Pat getting to know the police or the sergeant in the barracks. He was at this stage already accompanying people to the station when he was requested by them to do so when they had to produce insurance or ID. So it was very important at the time to have a name to contact when something like this happened. This proved dangerous as well for him as a councillor and for us as a family, and I can tell you honestly that there were threats made to us on many occasions. He was told to stop and called a Quisling and traitor and many other names I will not repeat. However, when I think back on those threats and how certain people tried to intimidate us, who in God's name were they thinking about? Certainly not the frightened young man in the police station. No, those people didn't care about anyone only themselves. Later on, the same approach was made every time a new regiment came into Forkhill and as the years went on and when the people, young and not so young, were being lifted and brought to detention centres for questioning, how valuable it was to have a name, someone to contact and to find out information for a heartbroken mother and father who could not even find out where their child was. Indeed Pat did not always need to contact each new regiment because on many occasions the Commanding Officer would come to speak to Pat and introduce himself. I remember on a few occasions when they called to speak with him the officer would leave his gun at the front door before coming into the house. Mind you, the gun was guarded by other soldiers outside. It was important to know the commanding officer of each new regiment because as well as problems which occurred concerning the attitudes of the soldiers at roadblocks there were other problems that could be sorted out very quickly when you knew who to speak to. Each year leading up to Christmas the local RUC would organise a Christmas function, when they would invite members of the community. These were people who were involved in many different ways with our local people, and they included local councillors, principal teachers, the Parish Priest, journalists, prominent citizens, and community groups. This was a way of getting to know these people and for people getting to know the RUC, in case at some time they needed their assistance where problems would arise, in whatever their day to day work involved. Of course this was not always acceptable, because many others, including the Provos were totally against it, but yet again it was good to have a contact in an emergency.

Our nights were in many ways associated with so many people. They will themselves remember all about it. Our phone could ring at any time of night and once a phone rings in the house everyone hears it. In our house, we heard it but our children heard it also. The times which I refer to are the times when our children were small and when the troubles in South Armagh were at their highest, when parents or people came troubled to our house at three o'clock in the morning. They were looking for Pat to make a phone call and try and find some information about a loved one. We were all up out of bed, every single tear, every single sob, every anxiety became part of us and we did what we could to help in a small way until the proper help was available.

I am very proud of the fact that my husband in his role as local councillor was there when he was needed, and that he did help so many people in more ways than will ever really be known. Down through the troubles the tension was high, especially in the little villages of

South Armagh, and every movement was monitored. Pat carried on at council level and I worked at home. I always kept my hand at hairdressing because I liked it and it brought in a little extra money and it also kept me in touch with people and I really did enjoy what I did.

Chapter 11
DODGY SALESMEN

The village and its people continued to go along with their daily work and routine and we were all aware of strangers. It was hard enough to cope with extra army on the streets and there were also in our midst some conmen. They came with bright ideas. For instance, they would offer to take your suite of furniture away to clean it and return it in a few days, and there were others who would repair your washing machine and bring it back in a few days. Some people did avail of these offers and were left without both. There was a lesson to be learned. A few months went by and one day this man called at the door asking if there was a vacuum cleaner which needed repaired and if so he could do it in one day, collect it today and bring it back tomorrow. His card had a photograph of himself and a phone number and it all looked ok. Word got around that this bloke was genuine and so more and more people gave him their vacuum cleaners for repair. Most of us living in Fairview at the time got repairs carried out. Then out of the blue, word went around that this bloke who was high up in the army, was going around collecting the cleaners and putting bugs in them and leaving them back and that every conversation or anything talked about could be heard by the security forces.

I remember one night both Pat and I being in a neighbour's house, and we were having great conversation with the husband and wife, when all of a sudden the wife jumped up and put her finger to her lips and lifted the vacuum cleaner which was sitting in the room and put it out in the hall. She came back in and said, "don't want them whores to hear what we are talking about!" When she told us what it was all about we split our sides laughing. Needless to say quite a lot of vacuum cleaners were left out in the shed after that.

South Armagh had by now gained a reputation as an area where murders, mayhem, harassment and intimidation were rife. The last few years had seen the deaths of many people in the area and the sealing off of the area by the security forces. The saturation of South Armagh by fourteen British Army battalions was contributing greatly to the suffering of the ordinary people of the area. It had led to the arrest of people totally innocent of any crime except residing in South Armagh, some of whom were over eighty years of age, and the raiding of homes in the early hours of the morning and frightening small children. It had led to the closure of border roads, an exercise that proved valueless. Most people from the area were working in the South and used these roads to get to their place of work. As soon as the roads were blocked, locals on both sides of the border got together and with diggers and lots of manpower reopened them.

Pat stated many times at council level that he was totally opposed to violence of any kind and even though he knew terrible things had happened in South Armagh, this did not give the security forces the right or excuse to treat everyone as terrorists, as they so called us. From my diary Monday 23rd January 1978 an extract reads: "Pat went to Newry, came home at 11-45 am. At 12-10pm exactly there was a mortar attack on the barracks. At first we did not know what it was but very soon the shock and the horror came, a day Pat nor myself will ever forget".

I heard the key turn in the door I thought to myself that Pat did not stay long in Newry. I went to put the kettle on to make a cup of tea for the two of us, and was walking towards the hall to reach the living room when we heard an unmerciful explosion. We opened the door to go outside to see what direction it was coming from and just across the road from our house we could see this object slowly twirling right above our heads as if it was in slow motion. The movements were so slow we thought it was not going to clear the roof of our house. At the same time, one of our neighbours had heard the explosion and had run out of her front door and was coming straight across the road screaming. She was half way across the road and Pat shouted to her to go back into the house and get down on the floor. She just stood there motionless. At the same time an old woman who lived in the corner house across from us (could hardly walk because of arthritis) was coming out of her gate. Again we shouted at her to get back inside her house but she kept coming on. Four of us were on the street with Pat trying to get one neighbour in to our house and me trying to get the old lady across the road when another explosion went off. In what seemed only a few seconds, we were in a state of panic. We managed to get the two women into the house. God knows where we got the strength to do it so quickly, but we did. As we got to the door the glass had gone from it and we got into the living room and then there was another unmerciful explosion, and so it continued for almost half an hour.

Glass was coming in all around us from our windows. The noise and then the silence and then the noise again. The old woman was sick and was throwing up and she just could not stop shaking. The other woman had left her door open across the road and was worried about what her house was like because at this stage the windows and the doors were twisted with the force of the explosions. Immediately our thoughts were with the children in the school. It was their dinner time and they would have all been in the dinner hall, which was mostly glass. As the school was in the proximity of the barracks, we knew the school would not survive in the force of the explosion. We were worried for all the children and for our own little girl who was just seven at the time. We rang an elderly man, Herbie Longridge who lived next to the school. The school at that time had no telephone and we asked Herbie to go to the school and find out if they were all ok. We also told him to tell the master not to let the children out of school until we could find out what the situation was.

The village was in turmoil. The fact that Pat was the local representative, when anything happened in Forkhill, either with the security forces or the Provo's, members of the press would contact him immediately. In this instance they arrived at our door and then the soldiers arrived and maintained that even though the attack was over they thought that there was a possibility that some of the mortars had not exploded, and they could be lying in some of the gardens of the houses. So they would have to move people out of their houses in order to carry out a search of the gardens. No matter when the attacks or the shooting happened, the policy of the security forces was to get people out of their homes. Either a mortar did not explode and it was better to get the people out so they could search the gardens, or perhaps bullets were lying around. It was terrible to move out of your house and upset little babies and children. The local people that day had been through enough and they did not want to leave their houses. Not only were the windows broken in most of the homes but the doors were damaged and could not be closed and there was no way anyone was going to move out of their homes, and anyway, they were all in shock.

The mortars were fired from a lorry that was parked at the lower part of the Fairview estate. Our house, that day, became a headquarters for all the reporters who turned up. We also had the soldiers still trying to convince Pat that they needed to get the people moved out of their houses. He had gone round and asked many people but they wanted the security of their own homes. Dear God, they did not even know if they were secure or not. A representative from the Housing Executive arrived at our house too as Pat had telephoned them. Many windows had to be covered and all the loose glass knocked out and anything that was dangerous had to be made safe. Then came the arrival of the police constable and the chief of police and as the reporters interviewed each in turn as to what damage was done, we found out that the only damage done was to the homes of the people of Forkhill; there was no damage at all to the barracks. The old woman from across the road was still with us. She would not go home. As we were all still in shock I kept making tea. That day I think I must have made enough tea to last a lifetime. The house was full and the reporters were doing as they always did. Get as much information as they could. In the meantime two other gentlemen arrived at our house. They came only to speak to the chief constable who was still there. They were from the forensic department, and were here to take fingerprints from the lorry from which the mortars had been fired. I remember they had white suits on them when they came in and one in particular was a very tall man. They left to go down to the lorry, and as they were leaving a very prominent and very distinguished reporter, asked Pat to go down and show him where the lorry was. This distinguished gentleman worked and reported for many newspapers, the main one being The Belfast Telegraph.

They all left together. Pat and his reporter friend came back, as did the two men from the forensic department and I asked Pat to go to the School to collect our youngest daughter as it was almost two o'clock and the children would be getting ready to walk down the road. I put the kettle on to make more tea and two policemen came in to report to their chief that they had the all clear to move the Lorry and then they left to do so. Pat was on his way out to get our daughter from school when next thing there was a loud explosion that rocked the village. The lorry had exploded as soon as the key was turned to start it. Then all hell broke loose. The children were just leaving the school and we had to get them stopped from coming down the road. The soldiers were letting no one move. We thought of all the children who must have been so frightened, for this was the second time in a day that they had been subjected to fear and disturbance. We managed to get Herbie who lived beside the school to tell the master to get the children back in and then wait until their parents came to collect them. After hearing what had happened, our reporter friend could not believe that only a few minutes ago he and Pat had walked around the lorry and it all got too much for him. I gave him a small sip of brandy to settle his nerves, but later we had to call a doctor and he was rushed to hospital with a heart attack. The fine big man who had just been around the lorry taking fingerprints did not look too good either and his face went pure white. Then I will always remember the young policeman who came running back to tell the Chief Constable that the two other policemen who started the lorry were injured. He had run through the gardens jumping the fences as he came. Then at the end of all that our little girl came in with her daddy, and the state that little one was in and I know that all the other children were the same. It was heart rendering.

Those little children had gone through so much that day. It was not fair that we all had been subjected to so much annoyance through no fault of our own. If those involved that day could only have seen those old people shocked and sick and the little children scared out of their minds, I wonder would they like their children or their mothers or their grannies in such a state. But then people who do these sorts of violent acts do not have any feelings.

My diary reads: "Tuesday January 24th 1978. The clean up begins.

All our houses destroyed with broken glass, doors off and in general a complete disruption. Housing Executive men came to repair the houses that were all badly damaged by the explosions. Four years after the first awful explosion which claimed a young life, it still goes on. To experience another attack like this would make me never want to live here. Please God, let it never happen. Thank God no one was killed."

It was very hard to settle after the mortar attack on our village but you have to go on and we did. It was not easy because now we had more army presence on the streets and you could feel the tension as well. Although we were not at all involved with these attacks, it seemed to the security forces that local people knew a lot of what was going on and we suffered because of this. The children were not long out of school and just starting their summer holidays, and by now the children of the village were very aware of the soldiers and they played their games and had their little camps. Our then youngest son and his friends decided that they would make a camp; this would be underground, a kind of dug out like what the soldiers would have along the country roads. There was waste ground behind the housing executive garages at Fairview and so they picked the spot where the camp would be and they started to dig. They put tremendous effort into this so-called dug-out and in no time it was ready. They had gone quite a bit underground and could actually get four of them into it at one time. Pat went into it and it was safe enough for them to play in and most of the summer was spent there. We knew where they were and they were not any distance from home. They decided to extend it, which meant that they had to make a little passageway so as to have more space to come and go. Now this little passage which they had made just touched the fence of a field which, when you got across the field and then through another field, led to the border. It would be very unlikely that anyone would use these fields as a means of getting to the border or to get to Forkhill and anyway children had been well warned never to go across the fields because of potential booby traps.

Early one morning our doorbell rang and I went to open the door and saw that our house was surrounded by soldiers. I could not understand what they would want. One came up the path and asked about the hole, which was behind the garages. Our house was just next to it and our garden was just alongside it. I explained about the children and how they played there most of the time, but one of the soldiers told me it was a risk to them and said that some one had been seen coming out of it. I told him that was ridiculous, that the only time it was used was by children. He asked me if I could prove this and I said that I knew because my son was one of the children who would play in it. "Then madam", he said, "you won't mind coming with me to look inside it". I did not mind at all as I knew it was quite safe and so to prove that point I went up to the dugout and looked in. Then he told me to go inside it, which I did again to prove a point. Dear God, what if someone had planted something in it? Mind you, it was something that could have happened, given the times we were living in, if it had, I was the one who would be dead. This is a small example of what could happen in Forkhill. The hole was demolished much to the dismay of our son and his friends.

These were difficult times for young people and indeed for everyone living in South Armagh. There were so many attempts made to shoot and even kill the security forces that even the smallest thing to us at the time had become a major threat to them. After that incident involving the dugout, which the children later had to fill in, was the end of their playing soldiers. That summer of 1978 was a very difficult one for everyone, parents and children alike. The children were restricted and were well warned to stay close to home and the parents could not feel content going to do shopping and leaving the children at home to be looked after usually by one of the older children of the family. There was always that awful fear of something happening while they were away and so under these difficult circumstances life went on in our village and our children continued to make the most out of their lives as they could. They went to school every morning, always surrounded by soldiers and they continued their lessons amid the noise of the helicopters continually landing at the barracks and taking off.

I had now started working in Jonesborough. There was a small hairdressing salon for rent and as Pat was at home during the day we thought we would give it a try, so I decided to work three days a week.

This would allow me some time at home and as my then youngest child was at school it suited me to work those few days and as I loved hairdressing and meeting people, it would be good to get me out of the house for a while. The residents of Jonesborough were lovely people and they made me very welcome and I must say I spent many great days there. I continued to work in my little shop for three years in all. It was situated on the hill just outside the village and I travelled to work in a little green Mini Cooper car, which Pat had bought very cheap. It was not great, but it got me from Forkhill to Jonesborough and home, and that suited me very well. Some evenings I might not be very busy and I could just pack up and go instead of having to wait for someone to come and pick me up.

There was a very strong support around that area for the Provos. We always knew that but it never caused me any concern working there, although they knew my husband was an SDLP councillor, and because during the time we were canvassing for the election we had come up against some, would be, tough men. There were a lot of very good people who lived there and also a lot of others who decided where you could go and what you could do and who would demand that you support their views with regard to what they said - right or wrong. However, I was in a position where I was working there but I was also providing a service to a lot of people in a way that was convenient for them. A treat for local women, for a short time at least. The joy of having their hair done and it saved them having to take a bus into town and wait a few hours to get a bus home. The days and the weeks went on and everything was fine and I would drive over on Wednesday, Friday and Saturday.

On one particular day it was quiet and I did not have many customers. It was during Lent and with Easter only a short time away people would hold back from having their hair done until nearer the holiday. I was sitting looking out the window when two men came from a field at the side of the little shop and walked straight over to a telegraph poll, which was just across the road. I continued to look through the window, passed no remarks of the men because there were a few farmers who had land with cattle grazing and now and again they

Chapter 11 - Dodgy Salesmen

would come to check the cattle. I turned away for a second, the next time I looked out I saw smoke rising and in the next few minutes the pole was on fire. This pole was just across the road from the door of the shop. There was no phone in the shop. A lady who lived a short distance up the road would allow me to use her phone sometimes in an emergency.

So I thought, my God I'll run up to her and phone someone but when I got to the door the two men that had started the fire were standing wagging their fingers. This was definitely a no. They were not letting me leave. I started shaking. I was completely on my own. What was I going to do and how was I going to get to my wee car to get home? I put the lock on the door and I sat down and I cried and I prayed that God would send someone to the door. The pole and the wires burned for ages and were still burning when thank God, two people who worked in the hotel at the bottom of the hill were passing and I went out. They did not seem to pass many remarks about the burning pole and just looked at it and walked on. I ran back in, grabbed my coat and keys and ran for the car and booted it home as fast as I could. I told Pat what had happened and we listened to the news to hear if anything further had happened but there was nothing. The next morning I had to go to work because I had appointments and I knew people would be waiting for me. Reluctantly I went. Everything was as normal. As if it had never happened, and no one said much about the pole that had been burned.

Saturday was a busy day and so my daughter who had just started secondary school would come with me to help and we travelled in the mini to Jonesboro and home. The following week after the pole was burnt, I went back to work and I was there only about half an hour when a big lorry pulled up outside the door and in it were workmen who had come to replace the pole. I had two people in the shop having their hair done, and the men hardly had time to put their feet on the road when next thing the lorry was in flames, and the workers were running away, down the road. There was no one about outside but I knew I was leaving for home, as my nerves could take no more of this. We gave the two women a lift back to their homes and my daughter and I went home. There were strange things starting to happen around me and I was not very happy. I never had much trouble while I worked there, but I had experienced pressure every Saturday evening when this young fellow would come in selling the Provo paper An Phoblacht. I would not buy it, Indeed many nights on our way home during the winter nights, my daughter would say to me that I should have bought the paper. She was worried that we would be stopped some night on the way home and made to carry a bomb in the car. This was the very real fear about proxy bombs

Chapter 12
PROXY BOMBS

It was around that time that the Provo's started using proxy bombs and indeed many times I thought they might put one in my car. As I was leaving Jonesboro and going to Forkhill I was passing the barracks every evening on my way home. But just like the paper I always said I would never drive a car with a bomb in it and they would have to shoot me on the spot. I always made that clear to Pat and to my children that I would never drive a car with a bomb. Indeed many evenings on our way home my little daughter would cry and say "aye, you might want to get shot but I don't". Later on when Flurry Bridge was in the news I could always remember my small experiences in my hairdressing shop just above it. I thought it might be better for me to find somewhere nearer home so that I could continue my hairdressing and not have to travel. And after a few months I did. We bought a caravan and put it at the side of our house and Pat converted it into a suitable place for me to continue working, which was great because I was at home if the children needed me. Now I was back in the village working among the community. I could hear first hand about what was going on around the village and I could let Pat know what people had told me, what happened to a lot of them on a daily basis. They could relate to me different incidents, which they had encountered with the soldiers The helicopters were now constantly flying in and out of the village, as it was now the only means of bringing in supplies to the barracks and the only means of transporting the troops out of the barracks, which they did many times during the day when they were about to set up roadblocks.

The frequency of the helicopters not only caused noise, but also created a problem for everyone in their daily tasks. One of the most annoying things was trying to hang clothes on the line in the garden when the helicopter was coming in to land at the barracks. It would swoop down so low you just felt that you wanted to cower down. It is such a frightening experience and so hard to explain but it was very scary when you heard it coming. You wanted to run back to the house. Then you thought that you might get the clothes up before it comes. You tried but couldn't, and then the down draught would send the clothes flying through the air. You couldn't catch hold of the line and felt so frustrated and annoyed that it became embarrassing. There was also the problem of the down draught blowing soot down the chimney and creating a complete mess in the room. I will always remember an experience when our youngest child, David, the baby of our family was just a few weeks old. I had him in a carrycot close to an alcove at the fireplace when the helicopter went over the house and the soot came down the chimney and covered the baby completely. It happened on a night that I had stayed up late to feed him before going to bed. I was so angry because his face, head and the clothes in his cot were destroyed. I picked up the phone in my annoyance and phoned the barracks to complain but I heard no more about it.

These were small incidents compared to the disturbances at night time. During the night the helicopters just seemed to come and go. There is nothing worse than to have broken sleep. The worst time was when a new regiment was arriving. I shall never understand why they always had to bring them in during the night. Pat did try to get some sort of explanation as to why this had to happen at night and also about helicopter noise in general. There was an enquiry and I shall give you all some of the answers he received. Firstly, I must explain here that when the British Army moved into the old RUC barracks it was a small building with very little accommodation, which they immediately started to fortify. They brought in Portacabins and erected a perimeter fence with sangers at each corner and at other vantage points throughout the village. At that time the army and the RUC were using motor cars, jeeps and lorries and some other armoured vehicles when moving along the roads of South Armagh. Apparently, because of continually being ambushed, when their vehicles were fired on and in some instances when there were landmines left along the roadside. Two policemen had been tragically killed from these landmines and it was decided by the army to use helicopters. So everything was transported to the barracks by helicopter and this included mail, all foodstuffs and all equipment required. When each regiment's term of duty ended and the next regiment was coming in, all these flights were at night-time and the constant comings and goings during these times was the greatest nuisance of all. Everyone in their houses was kept awake by the noise and at that time the explanation from the army was that because of the threat to police and army personnel it was much safer for them to use helicopters.

Pat was not satisfied with this explanation and so he brought several resolutions before the council as a local representative, on behalf of all the people living in the area who complained about the constant helicopter noise. Alas to no avail. He was told that this was known to be "Crown noise" and there was nothing could be done about it. However, he persisted and brought more resolutions before the council. Eventually, after a lot of pressure put by him to council, and with the support of other councillors there came some answers. Through the intervention of Seamus Mallon MP, because of a record in Hansard about crown noise at military airfields in England where residents were compensated, he asked why residents living with crown noise in Northern Ireland could not be compensated in the same way. Eventually some residents in the flight path in Bessbrook, Crossmaglen and Forkhill received a grant towards triple glazing for their homes. Newry and Mourne District Council Environmental Health Department Noise Survey, Noise from Military Helicopters, Bessbrook, Crossmaglen, and Forkhill 1988. I will now quote some of the findings from this report; Military Heliports have been established in predominately residential areas. Complaints about the noise from helicopters, low flying and the fear of accidents occurring has been received from many residents. In particular several residents have expressed concern about the effects on young children who are terrified by the noise when helicopters fly low over their houses. Among the areas where complaints have been received are Bessbrook, Crossmaglen, Forkhill, Kilkeel, Newtownhamilton and Rathfriland. I will give the Crossmaglen report.

The Crossmaglen Report notes that at every measurement site without exception, values of LAmax were recorded in excess of 82 dB (A). Maximum levels up to 101.6dB (A) were recorded.

The section "Local Reactions to noise" states:
"One of the most frequent complaints of residents, some of whom accept the noise to which they are exposed with considerable tolerance, is the disturbance which results from night flying. Again, on occasion, helicopters fly directly above some dwellings and at such a low altitude that residents fear their dwellings are going to suffer physical damage. One incident mentioned by residents involved a helicopter shedding its load, which dropped onto the roof of a building at the corner of the Town Square causing considerable damage. During the survey the army platoon based at the police station was changed and it was claimed by residents that this took place overnight. The residents indicated that there was considerable sleep disturbance over several hours whilst this operation took place and consequently the residents expressed their resentment of what they felt was an unnecessary disturbance. Incidents of this type must evidently lead to an increase in annoyance felt by residents and should, where possible, be avoided."

I will now give you The Forkhill report, this report states:
"Out of the 145 hours when Helicopters landed or took off there were 102 occasions when LAmax exceeded 82 dB (A). Indeed the range of LAmax values recorded was from 68.0 dB (A) to 99.4 dB (A) with levels in excess of 90dB (A) at every measurement site"

The section "Local Reactions to Noise" states:
"One of the most frequent complaints of residents, who to a large extent accept the noise to which they are exposed with considerable tolerance, is the disturbance which results from night flying. Again, on a regular basis, helicopters fly directly above most dwellings and at such a low altitude that residents fear their dwellings are going to suffer physical damage. The occupant of a dwelling at site 8 complained vociferously that low flying Helicopters had damaged his roof. Again, a resident in

Michael McCreesh Park stated that helicopters fly so low in that vicinity that, on one occasion, his television aerial had been broken. It was evident that the paintwork of many of the Housing Executive dwellings either in Fairview Park or in Michael McCreesh Park, close to the helipad, had suffered discolouration. The residents claimed that these dwellings had been painted within the previous year."

"A particularly annoying occurrence, in the residents' opinion, was landings and take-offs during services in the local catholic church, which is of timber construction and consequently has poor sound insulation. Incidents of this type must inevitably lead to an increase in complaints from residents and should, where possible, be avoided."

The work going on at the barracks became of great interest to a lot of the young people, especially the children, although they were told time and time again to stay away. The activities of the soldiers and the tanks and various armoured trucks that had been brought in by helicopters, were just too much to ignore. Tonnes of sand had been brought in and the Army were filling sandbags to help fortify the barracks and to a lot of parents' astonishment, quite a few of the children were discovered one day helping to fill the sandbags. Of course at this time we were not experiencing what was going on in Derry but it would not be very long before we would. It took almost seven years for the work, on the barracks to be finally completed. What started as a small extension to the barracks to accommodate soldiers moving into the area, became a huge army base as more and more troops were moved in. As well as the troops moving in and work becoming more and more regular, army trucks and tanks were also coming, and again this was of great interest to our local children and no matter how hard parents tried to keep them away from the soldiers that was where they could be found.

Chapter 13
FIRST MASS
IN FORKHILL

In Forkhill we had no chapel of our own and we went to either Mullaghbawn or Dromintee, which were our neighbouring parishes. Some people would go to Dundalk. Both churches were just about two miles from Forkhill and it was great to have them so close. But there were some who did not have a car and others who were old and could not walk the distance to either church. Time and time again people would voice the need for a church in Forkhill. A new priest, Father Begley had only recently arrived in Mullaghbawn. A nice man, very easy to communicate with, and whom Pat had been friendly with since his arrival in the parish. Pat was involved with the parish council. A group of people from each church in the parish, which included Aughanduff and Mullaghbawn, and who would help and advise the new priest with regard to fundraising and other things relating to the parish. It was after one of these meetings that Pat mentioned to the new priest how the people of Forkhill would dearly love to have Mass in their own village on Sundays.

To Pat's surprise he was very interested and asked if there were any buildings that would be suitable. There were two such buildings, the community centre, which was on Main Street, and the Irish National Forrester's Hall that was directly opposite the old RUC barracks. The community centre was on the first floor of the building whereas the Forrester's Hall was on the ground floor. The priest said he would have a look at them both to assess their suitability. It was on a Wednesday night and when they got to the community centre the weekly game of bingo was in session but they were able to see through a glass panel, which was at the top of the stairs that the actual room was not large enough to hold Mass. So they went next to the Forrester's Hall and decided that this hall was the most suitable. Then Father Begley said to

Pat: "Right. We'll start on Sunday". Shocked but delighted Pat said there was a lot to get prepared, to get an altar ready and arrange seating. Not forgetting that there was a Bar in the hall which opened at twelve o'clock on Sundays. Father Begley commented that from now on the Bar would open at one o'clock because he would say Mass at twelve starting the following Sunday.

A local committee was set up immediately and the work that took place was unbelievable. An altar had to be made, one that could fold up when Mass was finished, and when all the necessary things were in place, our first Mass ever to be held in Forkhill was said in the INF Forrester's Hall in July 1980. We had everything that was needed including a lovely choir of which I was proud to be choir mistress. That was how we got our Mass in Forkhill.

This was the making of history in more ways than one, given that soon afterwards Mullaghbawn church was being renovated. So christenings were being held in Forkhill and Aughanduff. Our first grandchild, Shane Patrick Toner was the first child to be baptised at Mass in Forkhill and the first baby ever to be baptised in the Forrester's Hall. There was a very lovely gesture from Margaret Thornton, Nee Shannon, when she gave me the flowers from the altar of that first Mass to bring into hospital and give them to my Mother-in-law Alice Toner who had gone into hospital a few weeks before.

With our Mass every Sunday in Forkhill and work still going on at the barracks, we were very concerned about safety when people were leaving the hall after Mass because while the soldiers were working, others were guarding the workers and were standing around with their guns. On one particular Sunday morning, as the people were leaving the Mass, one of the soldiers was at the wall outside and he started training his sights on each person leaving. Pat went over to him and asked him to stop pointing his gun as the people were leaving Mass. He became very nasty and was very abusive to Pat and told him that he, the soldier, could do, as he liked. After an exchange of words Pat moved on and said he would do more about this, which he did. He went to the major in charge of the regiment and explained his concerns as to the safety of the people. There were also reconnaissance helicopters in the mornings and always on Sunday at twelve o'clock and of course Mass started at that time and the noise of the helicopter drowned out the voice of the priest. This was another request Pat made to the major and was given an assurance that the helicopter would not fly over the hall between twelve and one o'clock, which it never did after that.

The major also said he would deal with the soldier who was pointing the gun, and did this in front of Pat. It was humiliating for the soldier as he saluted the major saying "Yes sir! No sir! I was only doing my job sir!" On the Monday morning as we were leaving the children up to school we saw the same soldier stripped to the waist and shovelling the biggest pile of sand I have ever seen and given that we were having a heat wave at the time he really was being punished. The sweat was pouring from his face and you knew by looking at him that this was hard work. We did not have any more trouble with the soldiers as we were leaving Mass. They continued with their work and left us in peace during Mass time. It was unfortunate that the other men of violence could not have been more understanding. They never missed an opportunity to attack the soldiers and of course what better way to do so, as they always did, than to use the local people as cover for their attacks. On one particular Sunday morning the soldiers were fired on as the people were starting to leave Mass and of course this brought them back out on the street again. Throughout the time the new base was being constructed, be it day or night, the Provos were active and indeed local people were in danger every time they left their homes.

Their children were also in danger. From where we lived in Fairview we all had to pass the barracks to go to the shops and to leave our children at school. This also applied to other parts of the village where people were also in danger. Imagine walking down past the barracks just as an attack was starting. You are in the line of fire and your first instinct is to get down on the ground and stay down until it stops. The soldiers were safe because they got behind the sand bags which they had to protect themselves and, there but for the grace of God were we, hearts thumping and legs shaking, getting up to run the rest of the way to get into somewhere for safety, while the people responsible scurried off not giving one damn as to the fear they put people through. This happened to me on two occasions. Once on my own and then with my two little children coming from school. It also happened to two old ladies walking down the street. There were many, many times when people and childrens lives were put in danger.

I remember one evening shortly after my late mother-in-law came home from hospital and was staying with us for a while. We had put a bed in our sitting room, as she was unable to go upstairs. She had got out of bed and was sitting looking out of the window when a burst of gunfire rang out. It was late evening and I ran from the kitchen into the room to try and get her away from the window. I was shocked at what I saw. Tracer bullets were coming from the Carricasticken Road, supposed to be heading towards the barracks but instead it seemed they were heading straight towards the houses in the Fairview Estate. The Carricasticken Road leads to the border and the attack lasted about fifteen minutes. They were well off their target and again, but for the grace of God, no one was injured. This was what we all had to live with. Lives were affected, young and old and it had become very difficult to try and lead a normal life. As my husband was an elected public representative, whenever anything happened in South Armagh, be it an explosion, a mortar attack, an ambush or a body found along the roadside, and we had plenty of those along our roadsides in South Armagh, reporters were on the telephone to Pat. They always had the information and they then would contact him for his comments. This always put him and us in very difficult situations. To comment on something without having the full information, but he did always condemn violence no matter what source it came from.

Times were still very difficult. Pat and I were very lucky to have a very good friend who had a mobile home in Rossnowlagh in Donegal and he offered it to us to go on holiday with the children. It was a very kind offer and we were delighted because so much was going on around us. We were just glad of the opportunity to get away from all the trouble. We decided we would go in August. The first week of our holiday in Rossnowlagh was brilliant, the pleasure of letting the children out and not having to worry about bombs or about shooting was great and the children spent most of their time on the beach and in the water. The weather was good and so we all made the most of it. The second week was not so good weather wise and we went to visit Bundoran, which was not very far away. We went to Sligo another day. Castles were always of great interest to me and wherever I travelled if there were castles in the vicinity, I would try to get to see them.

On our way back from Sligo I saw this castle high up on a hillside. It looked familiar and I recalled reading about it in a magazine, so I asked Pat to drive up to it so I could get a better view. We went off a side road that brought us to the back of the castle, and as we approached it we saw a British flag flying from the mast. It suddenly dawned on me that this was Classiebawn Castle, and I had read that every year members of the Royal Family would spend their holiday there. We could not get near it but from a distance we could see it. We then drove down to Mullaghmore to have a look around the little village. It was beautiful and such a peaceful little haven. The next day we were going home so we decided to spend the morning on the beach and leave late afternoon. It was a beautiful morning, August 27, so we packed up and headed down to the beach to spend as much time as we could before going home.

We were in the water and there were a lot of others as well, when this unmerciful rumble seemed to actually move the sand from under our feet. It was a strange sensation. We were a bit concerned as this was quite unusual, so we left the sea and went to the car, changed and headed for home. We arrived home around six o'clock and when the news came on we heard what had happened. Lord Mountbatten, a cousin of the Queen was assassinated by an IRA bomb, which exploded on board his pleasure craft in the sea off Mullaghmore. That was what we felt in the sea in Rossnowlagh earlier that day. Three other people were killed with him in the explosion. The device contained 50lb of explosives. The same day eighteen paratroopers were killed in an IRA attack at Narrow Water Castle in Warrenpoint. We were home and things were not getting any better.

In Newry and throughout the area after those killings, the graffiti appeared "Bloody Sunday not forgotten. We got 18 and Mountbatten". For the republican movement this had been revenge for Bloody Sunday in 1972 when members of the Parachute Regiment had opened fire during a riot after a Civil Rights demonstration in Derry killing 13 people.

Throughout the Troubles from 1973 we learned to live with the most terrible atrocities, day-by-day, week-by-week, month-by-month, year-by-year. The killing of 13 people in Derry and 18 soldiers at Warrenpoint and the Mountbatten family and friends on holiday at Mullaghmore, killed by two separate explosions on the same day. Here we have a grandfather, fathers, sons, brothers, all may I say loved ones, people who shared their lives with their loved ones. A terrible tragedy, and I know that a lot of people around South Armagh felt for the mothers and fathers, wives and children of those who were killed that day, as they did for every other person killed during those terrible times. I know for definite that there were people from South Armagh sickened by what has happened over the years. Our area was used so many times to dump bodies. To degrade a human being. To create heartache for their loved ones and most of all to deprive their loved ones of being able to give them a decent burial.

Here I refer to the disappeared. We sometimes feel anger when some thing terrible happens. At that moment we can move mountains with our anger. Why should we let it subside? Is it fear? We have lived with fear in South Armagh. The brave bully boys reminded us many times to watch what you say but the one thing that must always stay in your mind is that you have a clear conscience and if there is something that in your heart you know you must do, then do it. Do it and have peace of mind. We had a great friend. An old man, and a very learned man, whose grandson was killed by the IRA. This young man was shot dead in the hallway of his mother's house, in front of her in Rostrevor, Co. Down. We spoke to his grandfather after the funeral. He was heartbroken and I will always remember his words. "The people who did this will die crawling up the walls of some institution, because in years to come their conscience will bother them and if they have children of their own they will look at them and feel guilt for the children they deprived of their fathers. For the mothers they deprived of their sons and the wives they deprived of their husbands."

Life must go on and so again the weeks turned into months and months turned into years and more and more security forces were moving into South Armagh with more and more killings. The security forces had our area of South Armagh saturated with soldiers and they were responsible for a lot of unrest. Throughout Belfast and Derry and indeed all of Northern Ireland, many atrocities had taken place. Our area was suffering badly. We had the Parachute Regiment and the Royal Marines and they were out to get the Provos and so the war went on. We were now approaching the year of 1981. Another four years had gone by and an election was called for the month of May. This was to be a difficult election given the fact that there were hunger strikers dying in the H-Blocks of the Maze prison.

The Hunger Strike was staged to secure special category status for republican prisoners in the H-blocks of the Maze prison, formerly known as Long Kesh. During the 1981 Hunger Strike ten IRA and INLA prisoners died. Bobby Sands went on hunger strike in March 1981, joined at phased intervals by other republican inmates. In the Fermanagh- South Tyrone by- election of April 1981 Bobby Sands stood as an anti-H-block/ Armagh political prisoner. This contest was caused by the death of Independent Nationalist Frank Maguire. With a lot of political manoeuvring all other Nationalist candidates withdrew leaving Sands the only Nationalist representative standing against Ulster Unionist Harry West. Bobby Sands won the election by 30,492 votes to 29,046 and was elected to Westminster Parliament as MP for Fermanagh South Tyrone. Bobby Sands died on May 5. This was a sad time in Northern Ireland and on the morning he died word spread throughout republican areas and widespread rioting broke out. Now, with a local government election - taking place in the next couple of weeks you can understand how difficult it was going out canvassing from door to door when prisoners were dying on hunger strike. Many people thought it was wrong that these young people should die but the Provo influence throughout the area was so strong that people feared to express their true feelings.

Every council meeting was disrupted by IRA protesters outside the council offices calling on councillors to leave the chamber in support of the hunger strike, and although they knew it was terrible, with the four year term coming to an end, winding up had to be done. On one of these occasions council meeting protesters called on the South Armagh councillors to leave the council chamber. At this stage two of the SDLP councillors from South Armagh, Pat Toner and James Savage excused themselves from the chamber and went to the gates of the council offices and spoke to them. Through the gates they informed them that they felt bad about the hunger strike and the suffering they were going through but felt that by staying within the council and representing their constituents they would do more good than walking out. The protesters did not accept this. The councillors returned to the council chamber and continued council business. None of the other councillors left the meeting either.

Eight years from the formation of the new Newry and Mourne council area, and now facing another election, it was time to look back on the achievements the new council had made and so the councillors toured the areas where the good work was done around South Armagh. These included the play areas and playing fields at Newtowncloughue, the play area and changing rooms and toilets at 'The Planting' at Forkhill, the play area at Conway Park at Mullaghbawn and on to Crossmaglen where the council had agreed to provide facilities and refurbish The Square. At each place they went the protesters were there with their placards objecting to the presence of the councillors while the hunger strikers were dying. It was a very difficult time for everyone and although people were feeling so sorry for the hunger strikers there was nothing they could do. There was a lot of pressure put on the community to come out and march wearing black arm bands, and indeed many people did not want to do this but again they were too scared to say no and that was how it was.

The election in May went very well as the councillors were all returned to the council with a few new councillors and after a short break another four years began. On May 21 1981 Raymond McCreech from Camlough in South Armagh died on hunger strike. He was only 24 years of age. As a young teenager he helped to deliver milk with our milkman and was well known around the area. Just before he died five soldiers were killed in an explosion not far from Raymond's home in Camlough. The first year of the 1981 elections and the following years were very difficult and very stressful. It was a time when there was an all time low throughout South Armagh. We had, over the last few years coped with the tragic deaths of the three Reavey brothers (Catholics), shot dead in their own home on a quite Sunday evening and then the Kingsmills tragedy, the next day, when ten factory workers (Protestants) were taken from their work minibus and shot dead. Then we had constant explosions and now young men dying. It was all very hard to take in. Leaving the house to do the weekly shopping and wondering what was around the corner or what or whom you were going to meet on the roads.

Chapter 14
DISAPPEARED

On August 16 Charlie Armstrong left his home as usual on a Sunday morning to collect an elderly woman from her home to attend Mass in Crossmaglen. He lived with his wife and family in Rathview Park, Crossmaglen. Charlie never arrived at Mass and has never been seen since. His car was found in Dundalk in the Republic of Ireland the next day. The whole community in Crossmaglen where I was born and reared, and Forkhill where I now live, were shocked, and our hearts went out to Mrs Armstrong and her family. His body has never been found and the Provos were blamed for his disappearance. Two other men from Crossmaglen, Sean Murphy and Gerald Evans, disappeared in similar mysterious circumstances. Sean Murphy's body was found in his car at Dundalk Bay but Gerald Evans was never found. What terrible tragedies for these poor families. The Dungannon based priest Father Dennis Faul also blamed the Provos for the abduction and killing of Charlie Armstrong. Father Faul said it was a very serious religious, cultural, and anti-Irish action to deny these people a burial. Of all the most savage and barbarous acts the Provos have committed over the years, this is the worst.

The heartache, the hurt and the terror installed in children's minds will last till their dying days. The poor unfortunates who were sentenced to death and their bodies dumped along our roadsides of South Armagh, were degraded in life and death.

Throughout the early Eighties when the new security base was built in Forkhill there were not enough telephone lines to cope with the many soldiers who were now accommodated in the new base. They of course had to keep in touch with their families in England, so for a period of about a year all of us in Forkhill had to share our telephone lines. Each household had to share with one another and that was not acceptable to us. Not only were the Provos putting us under pressure, the security forces did the same and in both situations we had no choice. We survived but many a conversation was indeed overheard from the young soldiers calling their girlfriends and others calling their parents and husbands calling their wives. I am sure that they overheard our conversations as well and we were delighted when we eventually got our own telephone lines back.

Over a period of time the Provos believed that the security forces were using the cover of the GPO now called BT and the NIES telephone and electricity services for surveillance purposes. This led to the abduction of personnel from both the GPO and the NIES for questioning as to their identity. It was believed by the South Armagh Provos that British Secret Services or British Army was using the vehicles being used by the engineers from the GPO and the NIES. As a result of these abductions the engineers from both companies were withdrawn from South Armagh border areas. However, some people from the republican Provos, who were building new houses, discovered that they could not get electricity or telephones. Going back to my days working in Jonesborough, electricity workers were always being threatened in the South Armagh area. My husband, as a concerned councillor in the area, was approached by people on behalf of members of the Provos to complain that they could not get electricity or telephone to their newly built houses. Pat, who was a member of the Post Office Advisory Committee at the time, raised the issue at a meeting of the Post Office about people in the area being unable to get telephones installed. Through the council he raised the issue about the NIES being unable to provide electricity to the same new properties in South Armagh. The word came back from both bodies verbally that because of intimidation, hi-jacking and abduction of employees, they could not supply the service required but if a guarantee could be given from the Provos that workers from the NIES and Post Office GPO would not be intimidated, abused or abducted, then both companies would look again at the situation. Pat passed that information back to the people who approached him on behalf of the Provos, and after a while got assurances through the person from the Provos that there would be no more harassment, intimidation or abduction of the workers. Within months, engineers from the Post Office and Northern

Ireland Electricity were in the area installing telephone cables and electricity lines and in fact extra crews were brought in from other parts of Armagh, Lurgan and Portadown. Unbelievable. Workers from these towns previously would not set foot anywhere in South Armagh

After the death of Bobby Sands, his election agent won his seat in another by-election and this paved the way for Sinn Fein to look towards a political future. At the Sinn Fein Ard Fheis, their annual conference, members voted to take local government seats in Northern Ireland. Newry and Mourne District Council was one of the first councils in Northern Ireland to share power with the Unionist tradition and indeed many, many times they were congratulated on how power sharing was carried on in those very difficult years. Time moved on and after a lot of magnificent work had been done it was election time again.

Sinn Fein was now contesting the 1985 elections after years of criticizing all those who took part in the local government elections. Here they were doing what so many had always said they should do. Instead of being critical of those people who went and took part and won their seats and worked hard at council level to ensure that all communities got the best help to bring them through very difficult years. The fact that Sinn Fein were going forward in such strength in this election, especially in the South Armagh area, was a relief to know that you could go to the polling station without the threat of bomb and bullet hanging over you. This was a major turn around. Even a conversion, but we knew that people would cast their vote for those who had a good record of achievements in the area over those last four years and who had a comprehensive programme planned for the future.

It was regrettable that Sinn Fein could only point to death and destruction, which indeed continued as they went out to campaign. The May elections of 1985 saw the return of the original councillors plus some Sinn Fein members. The first official duty of the newly elected councillors is to select the chairman of council who will, when selected, preside over the meetings of the full council for the coming year. The selection is made by each councillor voting for the person they want to be chairman regardless of which party they represent. The full council were unanimous when they voted for Pat Toner of the SDLP to be Chairman of Newry and Mourne District Council for 1985-86.

Newry and Mourne Council area was not yet classified as a borough or city therefore the chairman was known as First Citizen or Chairman and not as Lord Mayor. It was a great honour for Pat and me as his wife. It was an even greater honour for me to be first lady and to accompany him during his term of office on most of his official duties. The first six months of his term of office was one of the most difficult times in the council chamber for any chairman of council. There was constant disruption at meetings with Unionist members walking out of the council chamber because of Sinn Fein involvement. Many meetings had to be adjourned because of the shouting of abuse across the chamber from both Unionist and Sinn Fein. There were times when Pat would arrive home from council meetings totally exhausted, and disgusted with the behaviour of grown men, who were supposed to be representing the people who had given them their vote; but Pat and the SDLP members of the council, with a lot of input from sensible councillors, got things settled down and the council worked as it always had done for the benefit of the people.

Throughout those difficult years of mortar attacks, bombings, shootings and abductions we always tried to keep a certain sense of normality throughout our communities. We all worked together to have one week in the summer where we could have a summer festival where everyone in the community could play an active part in making it successful both for children and grown ups. It was a time to try and forget the awful times we were living in, and we made it clear that we were determined for once that the men of violence were not going to stop us. I must state here that our youngest baby born in 1980, was now five years old and given that we had a very busy year, ahead, we brought him with us whenever we could. We always made sure he was in safe hands and given that there was ten years between our last daughter and him it was a new challenge. And, I must say we had some great times. Yet still, we lived in fear that somewhere along the way the men of violence would try to disrupt us. Thank God it all worked out well and for one week in the year our festivals went ahead. June was the Newry Canal Festival week and so the newly elected Chairman of Newry and Mourne District Council officially opened the Newry Canal Festival. It began with a parade, which consisted of marching bands and floats with all the different sports groups, drama groups, football and youth groups, including boat races and bathtub races on the canal. There were the Bonny Baby and Little Miss Newry competitions, which I had the pleasure of judging as the wife of the chairman and all of the week was a wonderful experience. Various art exhibitions and nights in local pubs where quizzes were held with the proceeds going to charity.

The South Armagh Festival was held in the last week of June and into the first week of July. Pat was chairman of the South Armagh Festival for many years and here he was to declare the festival open as Chairman of Newry and Mourne Council. It was lovely to see all our local people coming to him to view the 'Chain of Office', which he wore on all his official duties. Many of the older generation were so taken with the chain as most of them never saw anything like it before, and when the little children came to look at it he would take it off and put it on them and say "now maybe some day you will wear a 'Chain of Office' like this". As I have said many times before, these festivals gave our communities a chance to forget the troubles and every one of the committee made sure that this was made possible. Again there was the judging of the little Miss Forkhill, I did not do this alone in Forkhill because I was living in Forkhill and knowing all the children made this a very difficult task. I thought it was better to bring in someone from a different area. There were some great nights during that festival week when Pat was chairman of council because we invited a lot of people with whom we had made friends from all persuasions and they were delighted with the warm reception they received from the people of South Armagh.

Newry and Mourne Council wound down during the month of July and there were no council meetings although the officials did carry out most of the important duties. This gave a little time for recreation and holidays so it was all go as regards visitors coming to the area. With Raymond Turley who was then tourist /recreation officer for Newry and Mourne District Council at the forefront, any visitors were assured of the best possible hospitality and welcome. In early August a group of American boxers came to visit the area, 150 members from Montgomery County Front Street gym boxing team and the Teamsters Union local. They came at the invitation of Seamus Mc Cormick and Eamon Maguire of the Sacred Heart Clubs of Jonesborough and Belfast. The American Boxers took part in a tournament in Newry Sports Centre against an international selection.

The tournament was organised by the Sacred Heart Club of Jonesborough. This was a brilliant night and the sports centre was packed and everyone who attended, young and old, enjoyed the night's entertainment. Newry and Mourne District Council held a civic reception for the boxers and officials who were visiting the area. This was held in the SS Schooner in Warrenpoint (later to become known as the Aylesforte House) and guests at the reception included the US Consul in Belfast, Mrs Eleanor Raven Hamilton and the Vice-Consul Mr Mark Norman. Raymond Turley, Recreation/Tourist Officer of Newry and Mourne District Council was MC at the reception and welcomed the guests to Newry and Mourne. In a brief speech Mrs Hamilton, US Consul, referred to the kind-hearted people of Northern Ireland and hoped that the visitors would experience the same willing friendship she had found. Pat remarked that this worthwhile visit could not have taken place without the initiative and hard work carried out by the Sacred Heart Boxing club and in particular Seamus McCormick. As the result of this visit he hoped many social and industrial links would be formed. Bill O' Farrell, president of the Teamsters Union local 500, Philadelphia handed over a framed letter of greetings to the Chairman -whom he addressed as Mayor - from Pennsylvania and a gift of The Liberty Bell, a replica from the city of Philadelphia. This takes pride of place on the shelf with many other token gifts, which we received during that year.

The Kingdom of Mourne Festival was held in August and we always attended this festival as there were some very good events including the Seafood Banquet. Kilkeel played host to its first-ever pipe band championships. Mrs Maureen Grant, festival organiser suggested a revival of the championship contest at the festival and so after a lapse of 20 years the grounds of Kilkeel High School proved a perfect setting when the 38 bands turned out for this colourful, musical spectacle.

Chieftain of the Day and chairman of Newry and Mourne District Council, Pat Toner was dressed appropriately in kilt and buckle shoes for the occasion. I, as First Lady presented the prizes. This was one of the most beautiful and most enjoyable events that we attended throughout Pat's year of office. To hear the beautiful music as it echoed throughout the mountains and the fields of the Mournes is something we shall always remember. I had tears in my eyes as I presented the prizes as each person came, first to Pat and saluted him as Chieftain but most of all it was the little juniors who came to collect their prizes and did exactly as the adults had done - stood and saluted the Chieftain--that really stole my heart. All through the week there were various other events which Pat as chairman had to attend and it turned out to be a very busy time. As one festival finished, another began. There was the Omeath Gala Week which we were invited to attend and at a dance in the Park Hotel the Gala Queen was selected and so the week kicked off with lots of events. A traditional Irish night. A wine and cheese party, darts, pool, snooker and the highlight of course was a medieval banquet at the Park Hotel. There was another memorable occasion when Pat was chairman of Newry and Mourne District Council, one which we were so delighted to be involved with. That was:[The Glen Dimplex Challenge Match] Presented by [Merchants Snooker Promotions] in Newry Sports Centre on Thursday,13th February,1986. Newry welcomed Champions Dennis Taylor, Ireland's world snooker champion and Steve Davis, England's three times winner of the title. More than a thousand people in Newry gave them both a tumultuous reception when they appeared at Newry Sports Centre and participated in an exciting nine frame exhibition challenge match. It was organised by the local Merchants Snooker Centre of Merchants Quay and sponsored by Glen Dimplex.

Chapter 15
TENSION AT COUNCIL

As July came to a close it was back to council business for the councillors and the officials. Indeed it was back to a much-disrupted council chamber for the chairman. From when he took office, the first six months were the most difficult of his term. All through the years from the formation of the new council in 1973, meetings ran very smoothly and all parties worked well together but now with Sinn Fein members elected and taking their seats in the council chamber, it created a complete chaos between the Unionist grouping and Sinn Fein members.

It was always a policy of Newry and Mourne District Council to condemn all acts of violence from every source. In a particular incident, a premises in Newry was bombed and a lot of damage was done but also the management and members of the staff were injured. At a council meeting shortly afterwards it was proposed by the Unionist grouping that the council condemn the bombing of the premises. Sinn Fein members would not support the motion of condemnation and this lead to a lot of angry exchanges between the Unionist members and Sinn Fein. One Unionist councillor in his anger stated that they surely couldn't be expected to work with people who claim to be "Daytime politicians who represent night time killers. And has it not been nauseating since the May elections to hear certain people on an issue such as tourism when everyone knows that not one hotel stands in the whole of our council area because they have been blasted away by the cohorts of these same people. Is it not nauseating to listen to certain people complaining about unemployment and lack of industry when everyone knows their colleagues outside have destroyed places of employment and with their intimidation any job creation chances, yet they weep crocodile tears for the unemployed."

"Has it not been nauseating to listen to certain people complain about health and social service cuts when hospitals in the area have been crammed with people injured, maimed or killed by these peoples' cohorts. How can we explain to those whom have lost loved ones because of the actions of obnoxious men represented on our council that we should try and work out our differences with them? It cannot be done, and I know I speak with certainty on behalf of our combined party grouping of Ulster Unionists and DUP that we are utterly, unquestionably, resoundingly and irrevocably opposed to Sinn Fein both inside and outside this chamber". The councillor went on to say, "I am certain we do not speak for ourselves alone but for all people of honour and integrity in this area, Unionist and Nationalist, Protestant and Catholic". The Chairman had a very difficult time trying to keep the peace. It was a terrible few hours with abuse being thrown across the council chamber at members. Eventually the Unionist members lifted their papers and walked out of the council chamber. This was the norm for those first six months and with the guidance of the chairman and officials and sensible councillors things settled down and council business continued.

Throughout the year the Chairman carried out various functions. There was - the Sports Personality of the Year award where the Chairman presented the awards. The Newry and Mourne Festival of the Arts which down through the years has brought many visitors to Newry and Mourne. Newry Feis, A delightful week of entertainment from all the schools, with verse speaking, music and dance where every performance was pure perfection from all the children and teenagers throughout the Newry and Mourne area. The Newry Drama Festival was always the highlight of the year. Many drama groups travelled to Newry and always received a tremendous welcome and Newry, as always, did them proud.

Perhaps the most memorable and remarkable occasion in Pat's year as chairman of the council was as a member of the SDLP delegation to Washington in October 1985 during the early moves for peace in the North led by John Hume. The National Democratic Institution made the arrangements in Washington and the visit took place in the lead up to the Anglo-Irish Agreement, which was signed the following month.

Among many meetings over the week long visit with senators and representatives and others keen to help resolve the situation in the North was one with then Senator Al Gore of Tennessee, later to become vice president of the United States, followed by a meeting with the House of Representatives Foreign Affairs Committee. The chairman of this committee, Lee Hamilton stated that if a satisfactory solution was reached on peace developments, his committee would act "very sympathetically and with speed" to the creation of a supporting funding project.

The group was later received by Senator Edward Kennedy who was wearing a Derry tie in a tri colour bedecked office and who was the essence of cordiality and good will.

The delegation were joined by Denis Corboy the EEC information officer for a meeting with the Friends of Ireland group under the chairmanship of Tom Foley and which included Eddie Boland, John Murtagh, Bill Lowery, Pat Williams, Joe Mc Daid, Kevin Peterson, Walter Kennedy, Frank Mc Closkey and Kirk O'Donnell, the Speakers Council. Among the subjects discussed was the possibility of aid in the event of an Anglo Irish Agreement.

Pat remembers vividly Tip O' Neill hitting the table right beside him to emphasise his point and saying that "if you people can work out an Agreement I am telling you here and now that as my parting gift as Speaker, I will make sure that there will be financial support". Tip also had some advice on how to win elections. First, you need a new candidate, second you need the right issues, third you need good workers and fourth you need the money. If you haven't got the money you can forget about the other three.

The SDLP spent the following morning at the Democratic Party Headquarters where there was a further reception and lunch. They were guests of honour and John Hume was the guest speaker. Ten embassies were represented including three ambassadors, several senators and congressmen and other dignitaries.

The next day the SDLP were hosts to a dinner for 70 people in the Lyndon B. Johnston room in 'The Capitol'. The official speakers were Senator Eagelson, Brian Atwood and John Hume and Senators Daniel P Moynihan and Ted Kennedy both of who made short speeches, Dan

Rooney also attended.

Later the Irish Ambassador Paddy Mc Kernan hosted a reception for the group and on the day before they left for Ireland had dinner at the home of a prominent member of the Republican Party, Judy Mc Lennan, where the guests included one of President Reagan's aides.

Looking back it seems incredible that the delegation were able to meet so many people in such a short time. People appeared genuinely anxious to learn about the NI situation at the time and were keen to contribute in some way to a solution. While these were early days in the peace process, that US visit in October 1985 showed the intensity of the work that was ongoing a quarter of a century ago to achieve a lasting peace in Ireland and the central role that John Hume, Seamus Mallon and other members of the SDLP played in that historic process.

Christmas was fast approaching and business as usual at council level still continued. The shootings and the bombings were also continuous. People tried to make the most of the Christmas season and carry on as best they could under the circumstances. We still had the roadblocks from the security forces and as I said before, 1985 was a very depressing year for everyone and especially for the people living in the border areas around South Armagh. During the Christmas season prayers were said in the hope that the coming New Year would bring in change.

A report in The Irish News on Tuesday December 31st read, "Provos slap ban on shops in War Zone". The Provisional IRA in South Armagh has put a New Year Ban on new stores in an area which they have described as a war zone, extending along a concessionary stretch of the Derry /Dublin road near Culloville village close to the Co. Monaghan border. It was confirmed that two leading businessmen from the Republic –who acquired property in the area for the establishment of different ventures –were directed to move out. It was also learned one of the businessmen concerned –who bought the site for a five figure sum close to the border, received a written request from the Provos at Crossmaglen to cease development work at the site. This was the start of 1986 and when these threats were made in any part of South Armagh whether you lived near the particular area or not, once it's South Armagh, it involves every little village and town throughout the entire area. And, as far as the security forces were concerned we were all tarred with the one brush.

More and more troops moved into our areas and because of the threats made by the Provos, security was stepped up. Road blocks were on a much larger scale than before when we could get by with producing a driving licence. Now it was a case of "get out of the car and stand along the roadside" while the car was searched. This in itself proved very frightening because wherever the security forces were, there was always the possibility that in some way, word would get around that they had a road block and believe me, standing along the road side with them searching through your car was not a very safe place to be if the Provos decided to have a go. Throughout the north of Ireland, Belfast and Derry and indeed many little villages like ourselves were witnessing terrible sectarian murders and as we listened to the news reports of all that was happening throughout our country, we hoped and prayed that soon something good might come from all the work the politicians were trying to do.

Chapter 16
ABDUCTIONS AND MURDERS, WATCHTOWERS AND LOOKOUT POSTS

Abductions and murders were starting to become an everyday occurrence and to wake up to the news that a body was found near the border at Forkhill or Crossmaglen or along the country roadside in South Armagh was not a very good start to any person's day. We thought of the poor soul whose body was left lying there and of the relatives who lost their loved ones in such a tragic way. Again this did not help our area and the people of South Armagh did not condone any of these barbarous acts. All we wanted was to be left in peace to get on with our lives and the lives of our children. When the old barracks was being renovated and later the extension and then the new addition, which was to become the security base at Forkhill, the security forces erected a lookout post on the top of Tievecrom Mountain. This mountain overlooks the village of Forkhill and its surrounding areas, and indeed the views from that mountain extend as far away as Drogheda in Co Louth in the south of Ireland. Pat always talked about the time when he was young how he would go up the mountain with his dog and sit there for ages looking over the village and had often told our grandchildren how he would some day take them up and let them see for themselves the beautiful views.

This was not possible now as the army had placed flares along the bottom of the mountain and these would send a signal whenever anyone approached. Where we had lived with the lookout posts at the top of our gardens we now had this huge military post over looking our village, into our homes, and believe me through our windows and even into our bedrooms. As the years went on and more attacks were made on the soldiers and their base, these posts were extended and massive cameras were placed on the various vantage points on the mountain and so on top of all else we had to put up with having no privacy. There was no use complaining because while the men of violence still continued to do what they thought they were best at, we here in our village had to try and make the most of our lives and those of our children. As the attacks by the Provos continued on the security forces more mountain top lookout posts were erected and so the Crosslieve-Carrive Mountain military post directly behind us in the village was refurbished and became a massive construction.

Equipment and materials had to be brought in a convoy of lorries and would arrive during the night and early morning. Noise from the vehicles and the unloading of the loads kept everyone awake during the night, and then the materials unloaded had to be transported by helicopter which continued on an ongoing basis for several weeks. We were in the flight path of everything being brought to the mountain top, all sorts of building materials were crossing our homes and gardens, dangling from helicopters. It was a very frightening experience. On many occasions over the years some of these materials fell from the slings and on one occasion goods from a helicopter fell into the school playground. It was a miracle, considering all the goods being carried, that no one was killed.

I remember one beautiful summer day we had put an inflatable swimming pool in the garden, we were there with our family and all our grandchildren when one of these helicopters flew over the garden. The pilot was flying very low and in my annoyance I got my camera to take a picture because he was flying far too low for safety. When I was about to take the picture the pilot swooped down towards me. I dropped the camera and thought that day we would all be killed. I must explain here that it was an offence to take photographs of helicopters or security bases, I rang the barracks to complain about what had happened and they took the complaint and later that evening I had a call from the MOD. They apologised for what had happened but I said that, had the helicopter crashed at that time it would have wiped out our entire family and all because an incompetent pilot decided he would teach me a lesson. Our areas were used by young pilots on training exercises. We found this to be true, when on holiday in Minorca a few years later, we met a young man who had been in the army and had served a term of duty in South Armagh.

He had since left the army but he did do his training here flying helicopters in and out of South Armagh. South Armagh was still in the news as there were more abductions and more killings. We all now wanted peace. We had enough of the threats, the murders and wanted our lives back. We prayed so hard that the politicians would come to some agreement and we marched in silence so many times and prayed with the hundreds of people who turned out like us to ask and show how much we wanted peace. So, when leading up to the talks and the Good Friday Agreement we watched the news and prayed that soon the politicians and all those involved would find guidance and help to realise that now was the time. What great emotion when on our television screens we watched as the announcement came that a peace agreement was reached on Good Friday. We breathed a sigh of relief that now we could pick up the pieces of our shattered lives.

Newry and Mourne District Council had twinned with Ennis in Co Clare and every year we would go to Ennis at the invitation of Clare Co Council. A lot of the Newry councillors would go to attend the Agricultural Show and had a Stand there to promote Newry and Mourne. This was always held on the 15 August every year and it was a very enjoyable weekend. And so on the 15 August 1998 we went as usual, The councillors all knew each other well due to the meetings they held at various venues in Newry and in Clare and during the show, Clare FM radio station held an outside broadcast from the show grounds. Pat and myself always sang a few songs especially at some of the functions. We were asked to sing on the radio and said we would and we did one song. When we finished the young presenter said to us that he did not want to say anything to us before we sang, but he had reports of something, which had happened in the North and was not quite sure how bad it was. We went back to join the other councillors and told them what we heard and went back to the radio van. Then we were told about what had happened in Omagh. There was complete silence. We were so shocked and I remember one of the Clare councillors had a niece who had got married that day and he had invited all the visitors from Newry to go to the Old Ground Hotel in Ennis where she was having her wedding reception. We were looking forward to going but now with what we were hearing from Omagh, it was the last thing on our minds. We went back to our hotel and we watched television as the events of that terrible day unfolded.

Chapter 17
"GOOD OVERCOMES EVIL"

It was too late to drive home but we all agreed to leave very early the next morning. I have never seen so many grown up men and women cry as I did that night. All we could do was just sit in silence and watch those heart-broken people. We all travelled home the next day and most headed straight for Omagh. The dark days that followed was so heart breaking and as the days went on only terrible bitterness could be felt for the men of violence who did such a terrible deed. We thought we had trouble but it could never be any thing like this. Out again on the streets in silence, people together to support the people of Omagh, hand in hand, and all denominations. It had to take something like this to make everyone realise that this was enough and so the troubles in our beloved country claimed more unfortunate lives. How sad that our prayers and hopes for peace had to end like this. There was a glimmer of hope. Good always overcomes evil and out of the goodness and kindness and support that was given to the people of Omagh and the prayers of everyone throughout the north and south of Ireland, there was light at the end of the darkness. After many years of waiting at the end of July 2005 the Provos formally ordered an end to its campaign and in August the government set out a two-year plan to scale down security. The following month, General John de Chastelain's decommissioning body said the Provos had put all its weapons "beyond use". There was hope for the future and again we hoped and prayed that soon it might all fall into place. Eventually it did. Soon after, the lookout posts began to come down. Crossmaglen began to witness the removal of the lookout towers on the outskirts of the town.

I used to get so angry when I went to visit my mother. I had to pass the Borucki Sanger named after a dead paratrooper. This was a huge construction over looking The Square on the spot where Jacks Hut stood and where we used to court on the way home after a dance in the Rangers Hall. Soon it would come down and slowly one by one they all came down and a sense of normality became possible. The building on The Square which was the Hibernian Bank- the one I mentioned where my Auntie Josie worked as housekeeper for the Bank Manager, and where I used to go to keep her company- was bought by the Carragher family and redeveloped as "The Cross Square Hotel". The little friend with the ambition, the one I mentioned from my school days, joined the Navy that year and there were two other young fellows went away as well. One joined the RAF and the other the British Army. I remember the first year they came home on leave and all looked very handsome in their uniforms. They had ambitions and only wanted to fulfil them. I think they came home once more but never again because of where they came from. Their lives were in danger and under threats from the people who dictated what you could and could not do.

I did finally get that chance to view The Square from those lovely big windows in the attic of the old Belfast Bank after it was sold and renovated. I rented a unit from George Loan to do hairdressing and one day he brought me up to the top rooms and I got my view of The Square, only to hear that while it was out of use, gunmen had gained entrance and shot a soldier from those windows as he walked along The Square.

The Rangers' football field is no longer over shadowed by the security forces, which occupied part of the ground as a military base for many years. It is now a venue where the brightest and best of football teams come to play. We are delighted to see Crossmaglen becoming so popular for good reasons instead of the bad publicity it got over the years and to see how throughout all the Troubles it upheld its strong GAA tradition, with Crossmaglen Rangers becoming All Ireland Senior Club Champions many times over.

Forkhill, our own village, eventually was to see the end of the lookout towers and the domineering security base, which over the years caused us great hardship and distress. At the moment, Forkhill is not getting the recognition it should for what we have all suffered over the years. Our social lives changed in ways that left us reluctant to enjoy life to the full. In our village we had two pubs, The Welcome Inn where throughout the troubles we had the festivals and The Ring of Gullion

CCE (Comhaltas Ceoltóirí Éireann) with traditional music sessions every Tuesday night and both suffered the troubles through their clients having loved ones killed but, throughout all those very difficult years they were a lifeline although they did not know it. We had The Slieve Gullion Inn with Mickey, Kitty and Babs Haughy, or Larkin's, as it was known. Larkin's is still very much alive, if I may say so. It is under new management, but like everywhere else the memories are there. These memories always bring you back to some good times. Throughout the Troubles it was always somewhere to go to have a chat with friends, it was that sort of pub, homely and frequented with friendly, kindly people. Many an evening when you felt a bit low it was to Larkin's we would go and in a few moments of entering the pub and ordering a drink, the conversation would start between whoever was there and in no time everyone was taking part.

The regulars included many wonderful people and sadly a lot of them have passed away, but their stories will live on, like those of Peter Vincent Murphy, a true gentleman, who told of his years as a young man working as a Pahvee in Canada and later in England and throughout Ireland. There was Tom Murphy and Neilie Casey, each an authority on Gaelic football, Paddy Gallagher and Des Campbell, the late Leo Garvey, Francis and Sheila Faughey, Paudric and Bridge McCoy, the late Junior Murdock, his wife Katherine, Jim and Olivia Carroll and many more who made life that little bit more carefree during those troubled times.

More than four decades on, and after the Good Friday Agreement and the restoration of the new Assembly, we here in Forkhill are left with the site where the security base was situated. There have been many proposals made by various politicians and our local people. It is the local people who have lived in a different South Armagh: for over thirty years when we had our lives terrorised by the security forces and the Provos. We would all hope that those in authority will ensure that the final project benefits local people, the population who have suffered so much over many years, and not become a speculators paradise that will make money for people who have plenty. The site should be converted to a park, with walk ways and areas where the elderly can sit and where little children can play without fear of bombs or bullets, and enjoy our picturesque village in the shadow of Sliabh Gullion, where our children can take their children and their children's children to all the places that they were deprived of in their youth.

Author's Note

It is often said, 'Never look back, look to the future'. However sometimes before you move forward, you need to reflect on the past. Many mistakes were made on all sides of the conflict, injustices have been done on both sides, and many lives lost unnecessarily. We need to work together to insure that what happened over the last four decades, will never be permitted to happen again.

Since starting to write my book a lot of things have changed, people whom I've mentioned have sadly passed away. Indeed many things that seemed impossible have been made possible. We were relieved for both families of the disappeared the Armstrong and Evans family, when their beloved ones were found and that we were able to attend their funerals.

I shed many tears writing this book, especially when reflecting about the atrocities carried out by all factions during those troubled years. We hope that eventually all the disappeared will be returned to their loved ones and that we will find the real peace we deserve.

Acknowledgements

I wish to take this opportunity to thank the many individuals who have assisted in bringing my book to fruition.

Peter Makem
Joe Coyle and Fiona Campbell
Seamus Mallon

Many thanks to Toni Carragher and Glen Print for the use of their photographs. To my family for their patience, perseverance and endless support, David and Maureen, what would I have done without your help when my computer skills failed me. To Sharina, Aoife, Shane, Enda, Sheila and Teresa for proof reading. Morgan and Oonagh for your encouragement. To Pat for the many times I interrupted him, watching his favourite programmes. A big thank you to all of you. Finally thank you, to Barry at BJ McNally Printers for cover design and typesetting of the book.